"The first time I met Andy, I knew I wanted to spend more time with this guy. The second time I was with him, I realized, *I'd better have a way of taking notes.* The wisdom he can spontaneously add to a conversation is awe-inspiring. Of the hundreds of really smart people I've met over the years, Andy is among the few that have earned the right to sit in the wisdom seat. His emphasis on relationships and how important they are to a leader are not only among his pearls of wisdom; they are values he clearly lives by. He's passionate about building relationships; he's good at it; and, he does it in the most natural, inviting way. In my book, he's a true pro."

Steve Hartwig, *CEO/Managing Partner,*
C-TEQ Data Consultants, LLC

"Andy does a masterful job of using his unique life and business experiences to communicate important leadership lessons. He has a God-given ability to learn from his experiences and the guts to openly and winsomely share what he has learned to help others. *Pro Leadership* is a great read for a rookie looking for a comprehensive source of leadership wisdom. It is also a great read for a seasoned veteran who would like to refresh and expand leadership his or her capabilities. I'm going to strongly recommend this book to my entire leadership team!"

Dave Bremer, *Managing Partner,*
Boulay Financial Advisors, LLC

"Andy, thanks for allowing me the opportunity to pre-read your book. My goal with business-related books is to grab a few pearls of wisdom. In the case of *Pro Leadership*, I found some great takeaways I'll use. Here are a few that resonated:

- the golf analogies—particular
- the culture discussion

- "It's not knowing, it's caring"—a good HR and sales message
- allowing EQ to lead
- Culture trumps strategy. Growth, freedom, openness. Do my people fit the culture? Does the culture fit the people? Do we have a people problem or a culture problem? Good stuff!"

Bruce Christensen, *Chief Executive Officer and Village Elder***,** *The Christiensen Group*

"Thank goodness for people like Andy Wyatt. He is a wise leader with a gold mine of experience, who has found his calling as a coach. I am grateful for the one specific conversation with Andy 12 years ago that changed me forever. If you invest the time, each page in this book will bring you insights to help you thrive."

Paul Batz, *CEO and Founder, Good Leadership*

"Perhaps it's because I know the person behind the story that I was able to read this listening to Andy's voice in the narrative. The book is genuine and authentic and I'm richer for having finished it. Yes, I finished it in two days. For the records, I have NEVER EVER read any book in two days, short of the *Green Eggs and Ham* variety. I tell you this because the book is a walking inspirational manuscript that challenges the depth of my leadership down to the toes. Thank you for sharing it with me. I'm never too old to learn and now I'm off to answer the question, 'What's My Why?'"

Andy Eckert, *Chief Marketing Officer at RexVid*

"This book is difficult. It will challenge your base understanding of leadership—your attributes—in a clinical manner demanding you examine the most complicated but critical component:

yourself. Yet Andy provides the simple, human touch to provide the needed guidance, and a gentle but firm hand of hope and courage to change."

Wiz Wyatt, *Managing Partner, Rourke & Company, LLC*

"I'm immensely thankful that my friend Andy Wyatt masterfully occupies the "wisdom seat" in my inner circle—he's a steady source of profound counsel and encouragement to me and many others as we tackle leadership challenges both great and small. What a gift to now have Andy's insight, experience, and wisdom boiled down to a very readable, practical, and adaptable book for leaders and leaders-in-the-making (that's everyone!). All who seek to grow in character, performance and credibility will benefit greatly from *Pro Leadership.* Find a quiet place, sit down with a journal, and just let Andy talk to you through these pages. You'll find your personal arc of excellence elevated to a new level."

Colonel Eric R. Bents, *USAF (Ret)*

"Andy Wyatt is very clear on his own personal why, which is *"to inspire and equip leaders who desire to develop the leader within and to become all they were created to be."* In *Pro Leadership*, he often uses the words "leader" and "entrepreneur" interchangeably; at its core, *Pro Leadership* is an entrepreneur's tool kit and manual for growing into the leader his or her dreams require. The juice is worth the squeeze with this important contribution to the dynamic field of leadership development. Its appeal is equally strong for the first time or serial entrepreneur, as well as those who are rediscovering who they are and pursuing second-half ventures."

John Mitchell, *Founding Partner and Retired CEO of Health Care Futures L.P.*

"In a world where we are drowning in intelligence, there is a dearth of wisdom. Andy brings honest, grounded truth that is so needed in today's world and workplace. This is a book that is a must read to lead in life and business, based on solid and wise counsel. Timeless truths for turbulent times."

Philip Styrlund, CEO, The Summit Group

"After an accomplished investment management career, Andy has articulated the guiding principles of leadership and success; very well done!"

Bill Spell, Spell Capital Partners, LLC

PRO LEADERSHIP

PRO

LEADERSHIP

ESTABLISHING YOUR CREDIBILITY,
BUILDING YOUR FOLLOWING,
AND LEADING WITH IMPACT

Andrew Wyatt

NEW YORK

LONDON • NASHVILLE • MELBOURNE • VANCOUVER

PRO LEADERSHIP

Establishing Your Credibility, Building Your Following, and Leading with Impact

Published in New York, New York, by Morgan James Publishing. Morgan James is a trademark of Morgan James, LLC. www.MorganJamesPublishing.com

ISBN 9781631951244 paperback
ISBN 9781631951251 eBook
ISBN 9781631951268 audio
Library of Congress Control Number: 2020935463

Cover Design by:
MTWdesign, Knoxville, TN

Interior Design by:
PerfecType, Nashville, TN

Morgan James is a proud partner of Habitat for Humanity Peninsula and Greater Williamsburg. Partners in building since 2006.

Get involved today! Visit
MorganJamesPublishing.com/giving-back

To inspire and equip leaders who desire
to develop the leader within,
in hope that they may become all they were created to be.

To Luann, my wife and best friend.
She believed in me when I did not.
She had confidence in me when I did not.
She supported me when I would not.
Without her this book never would have never been written.

TABLE OF CONTENTS

Foreword		xv
Introduction		1

Establishing Your Credibility

Chapter 1	The Entrepreneurial DNA	7
Chapter 2	A Foundation for Leadership	17
Chapter 3	Know Yourself	27
Chapter 4	What's Your Why?	41

Building Your Following

Chapter 5	It's All About Relationships	51
Chapter 6	Leadership Creates Culture	65
Chapter 7	Allow Your EQ to Lead	77
Chapter 8	Be a Motivator	89
Chapter 9	Teach What You Know	101
Chapter 10	Be Real (Lead with Integrity)	111
Chapter 11	First, Lead Yourself	121
Chapter 12	Praise in Public, Correct in Private	131
Chapter 13	Be Willing to Take a Back Seat	141

Leading with Impact

Chapter 14	Leave Room for Providence	151
Chapter 15	The Downside of Consensus	163
Chapter 16	Communicate³	173
Chapter 17	Decision-Making at the Speed of Business	183
Chapter 18	Leave Yourself Options	193

CHAPTER 19   Margin Is Magic   203
CHAPTER 20   The Wisdom to Diversify   215
CHAPTER 21   The 45-Minute Meeting   227
CHAPTER 22   Embrace Your Failures   235
CHAPTER 23   Major, Don't Minor   245
CHAPTER 24   Win Today   255

AFTERWORD   265
ABOUT THE AUTHOR   269

ACKNOWLEDGMENTS

One of the most commonly heard labels in leadership circles is "self-made." In fact, I haven't met a leader who at one time or another didn't consider themselves self-made. I will never forget the first time it was applied to me. I was speaking, and as part of the introduction the person introducing me said, ". . . and he is a self-made man." I felt proud to have been recognized in this way. Today, however, I regret it took me so long to realize what a lie that was. Getting knocked off my high horse and having to take a hard look at myself and my life helped me to understand there is no such thing as a self-made man or woman.

Nothing proves this more clearly than the process of writing a first book. As I look at the manuscript sitting on my desk, and I consider the hundreds of hours spent writing it, I can also see the faces and hear the voices of the countless people who helped me along the way. Together they get the credit for the form and flavor of this work.

I am grateful for:

- Bev Johnson, the world's greatest therapist, who saw my list and said, "I think that would be a good book; you should write it."
- Thom Berkowitz, my friend, who saw the list and said, "This would make a good book, you should write it."
- Dennis Trittin, without whom I would not have built the business that taught me so many of the principles that follow, and who read the original manuscript and encouraged me to meet his publisher and editor.

- Arlyn Lawrence, my publishing coach and editor, who read the original manuscript and had the courage to speak the last ten percent to me when she said, "If we can get the chip off your shoulder, it would be a good book." Then she stuck with me, helped knock the chip off, and helped turn an amateur into a pro. Arlyn and her team at Inspira are real pros.
- Dave Frauenshuh, my friend and mentor, whose grace and generosity made this book possible.
- Jay Coughlan, my coach and my friend, who encourages, inspires, and equips me along the way.
- Dave Bremer, my friend and trusted advisor, who always reminds me: you can't take it with you.
- Scott Slater, my faithful friend; everyone should have an English major in their inner circle.
- My Band of Brothers, who every week listened to me whine about this book and encouraged me to keep going.
- My Brother Wiz, my only brother, but better yet, my friend, a natural leader, a real pro, who helped me distill the pro-leadership principles in this book.
- Loren Kix, my dear friend and wingman, who makes me desire to be a better leader and man.
- Claire, Joe, and Maggie, who listened to my stories and always said, "Way to go, Dad; we love you."
- Luann, who said, "I want you to write the book," then, "I think it's time for you to get an editor."
- Too many others to mention. I have a word and page limit on this work, but as our paths cross in days ahead, be assured, I will recognize and thank you—because I have learned I was not self-made.

FOREWORD

"Are there any shortcuts to success?" This is my favorite question to ask audiences during my leadership workshops. Judging by their lengthy pauses, they clearly think it's a trick question. In the end, only about a quarter raise their hands, probably because the word, "shortcut" often has a bad connotation. *But, not in this case.*

The answer, of course, is, "Yes"... by immersing yourself in the wisdom of great leaders. In doing so, you learn invaluable lessons from their successes, failures, and mistakes. And, if you have the privilege of a personal relationship, you can seek their feedback, too.

In *Pro Leadership*, you are about to experience such a shortcut. One that will position you for a lifetime of leadership excellence—provided you take this gift of wisdom to heart. It comes courtesy of an admired man, a great leader, and a natural coach whose heart is to see your leadership flourish to levels you may never have thought possible.

Before becoming an author and publisher, I was blessed with a twenty-seven-year career in research and portfolio management at Russell Investments. Among my greatest responsibilities was to evaluate the leaders of thousands of investment firms around the globe. It was an incredible perch from which to gauge the habits of the best and brightest. And, it was there that I met my friend Andrew Wyatt, who clearly fit the bill. At the time, he was leading Cornerstone Capital during its heyday.

Now, years later after enduring some formidable, gut-wrenching challenges, Andy is fully equipped for his most important work—sharing his leadership wisdom through this book and his coaching practice.

Andy offers you a refreshing, holistic, and compelling vision for leadership that encompasses mind *and* heart. Unlike the impersonal, task-driven, and control-oriented approaches so common today, you will be treated to new perspectives that empower and build motivated followers committed to a worthy vision. Through self-discovery and reflection, you will learn to live in alignment with *who* you are and lead accordingly.

In *Pro Leadership*, Andy displays an uncanny knack of selecting some of the most vital and challenging topics the best leaders evaluate:

- How can my leadership foster a culture of excellence and inspire, empower, and motivate my employees?
- What are the most important leadership qualities for me to model?
- How can I develop my Emotional IQ to build strong relationships and communicate effectively with my employees?
- How can self-discovery help me define my purpose, identify my unique assets, and create my pathway to fulfillment and legacy?
- How can I organize, prioritize, and execute to turn my vision into a reality?
- How can I improve my decision-making effectiveness under uncertainty, urgency, and internal disagreement?

These topics and others make this book a relevant read, with valuable insights you can apply to all areas of your life.

(Just wait and see how it will make you a better family and community leader and friend!) I recommend you "go deep" with yourself when reading *Pro Leadership*, by thoughtfully considering its reflective questions. You will reap the greatest rewards this way.

Our world needs more leaders and coaches like Andy Wyatt. I encourage you to share this deserving work and message far and wide with your colleagues and friends.

Thank you, Andy, for sharing your heart and mind with us and for helping us become the best leaders we can be.

Dennis J. Trittin, CFA
President and CEO, LifeSmart Publishing
Author of *What I Wish I Knew at 18*, *Parenting for the Launch*, and *Wings Not Strings*

INTRODUCTION

"What would you do for free?"
—Bob Hobert

> **PRO LEADERSHIP PRINCIPLE:** Pro leadership is a journey, not a destination.

It was the summer of 1985, Ronald Reagan was the President, and I was twenty-four years old and a straight commission salesperson, fresh out of college, trying to figure out what I wanted to do with my life. My dad helped me to get a sales job, and I was having a measure of success. The job was meant to complete my "education" by teaching me some real world lessons I could not have learned in college.

But I had a nagging feeling, *This isn't it.* Straight commission sales wasn't what I was made for. That nagging feeling led me to Bob Hobert, a world-renowned industrial psychologist and the father of my oldest and closest friend. I considered Bob my second father, and his three sons my brothers.

I will never forget the day Bob took me to lunch at the Minneapolis Club, that old-line, ivy-covered club in downtown Minneapolis where business was "done." Bob knew me better than I knew myself. He had been "shrinking" me since I was in the first grade, so it didn't take long for him to get to the point. "You don't like your job."

"Well," I said, "that's not entirely true."

1

"No, no, that wasn't a question, that was a statement. You don't like your job, because it's not right for you," he replied.

"Why don't you think it's right for me?" I asked.

He looked me straight in the eye, and said bluntly, "Because you are not really money-motivated, and although this job pays you well, the money is not enough to continue to motivate you."

Checkmate. In one sentence he had summed up what I had been wrestling with but could not figure out. I didn't know what to say. It was the truth, and sitting there I understood it for the first time. So, I asked, "How do I know what's right for me?"

"What would you do for free?" he asked. "Now, go and figure out how to get paid to do it." I will never forget his advice, even though it took me thirty-two years to apply it.

You see, the business I had founded and built my life upon had come to an unexpected end and, as a result, I needed to start over. But where? How?

Thirty-three years of business experience, lessons learned, and wisdom gained had changed me. I was no longer the young kid sitting across from the wise psychologist. But those years and circumstances had prepared me to accept his advice. I was ready now to answer the question, "What would I do for free?"

It was a cold November day, eleven months after I had turned the lights out on the company I built. Its ending didn't leave me with enough money to retire, but it did provide me with some time to figure out the answer to Bob's question. I had been invited to speak to a business group at a luncheon meeting in a Midwestern college town, a five-hour drive from my home. My days of private flight were over, and commercial wasn't practical, so I drove.

Since ending my business, I had been exploring various opportunities and trying to figure out what I would do for free. At the same time, I was loosely mentoring, one on one, a small handful of entrepreneurial CEOs. Since my speaking commitment required ten hours of driving, I scheduled four "coaching" calls: two for the way out and two for the way back. I loved those calls and was energized by the interaction with these leaders. It was clear from the way they spoke to me that our time together was valuable, and all were eager to set up our next session. I arrived for my luncheon speech invigorated from coaching, hardly feeling the effects of my two hundred and seventy-five-mile drive. I was having fun.

The speech was one I had given before: "Without Leadership, Nothing Happens." It was roughly forty-five minutes, comprised of personal experiences, my testimony, and stories of my life building a business and applying the wisdom I had learned along the way. Meant to inspire and equip those who hear it, little did I know that it would become the root of this book.

After my forty-five-minute talk and thirty minutes of Q&A, I was back in my car for another five-hour drive. I skipped the lunch—I'd rather have McDonalds. While I sat eating my Number 3 Value Meal and drinking my Coke, I was thinking about the speech I had just given, the coaching calls that morning, and the two upcoming ones scheduled for the drive back. I had just spoken to a room full of people in a hotel ballroom. I was only acquainted with the few people who invited me, and I would probably never cross paths with the majority of my audience again, but I felt the weight of my words and the humility of knowing so many people had come out to hear someone who had failed in business. I was struck in the same way by the men I was mentoring; they were trusting me and in my advice to them. They were applying it and expecting positive results.

This is when I first realized I had moved to the wisdom seat, that seat at the table where your experience, both good and bad, has worked itself out in your life. The lessons you have learned and the wisdom you have gained, will (if you allow them) be a help to others who have not yet been where you have gone. As I drove, I considered all this and came to the conclusion I needed to go pro.

Yet, even though several others considered me a "pro leader" and speaker, I did not. But I wanted to be. So, as I drove, I contemplated the place where I found myself—i.e., the wisdom seat. I loved it, sharing my experience and the wisdom I had gained was helping people. Suddenly it wasn't just about me and my P&L; it was about inspiring and equipping others to be the leaders they were meant to be.

With two ninety-minute coaching calls scheduled during my five-hour drive home, I had two hours to ponder the question, *What would I do for free?* The answer came to me: just what I am doing now—writing, coaching, speaking, inspiring, and equipping others to be all they were meant to be.

So thirty-three years after Dr. Hobert asked me the question, "What would you do for free?" I had the answer. Now, I only needed to answer his second challenge: "Figure out a way to get paid for it."

Although I was coaching leaders, at the time I didn't realize I was doing it. Why? Because when I was a CEO, my coach was a Harvard PhD psychologist, and that wasn't me at all! In contrast, my version of a "PhD" was from experience, hammered out over a thirty-three-year business career.

I decided to do some market research. I spoke to the leaders I was already mentoring and asked, "If you were going to hire a coach, would you want a PhD psychologist, or someone who has been where you want to go and could guide you there?" It was unanimous; everyone chose experience over education.

My revelation led to a twelve-month period of research and development in the field of professional coaching. I sought out high-level leaders and their coaches, who most graciously shared their insights and experience. They also gave me advice and answered the one question I asked them all, "If you were starting again, is there anything you would do differently?"

This book is largely the result of their combined advice and of my own observations. In the world of leadership development, there are two basic types of people: those who use material created by others, and those who create their own material. Maybe it's because I have a strong creative streak or simply that I have entrepreneurial DNA, but I found myself attracted to those who created their own content. Not surprisingly, they were also the ones who were working at, and in, the highest level.

So where to start? Pro leadership always starts with the leader, and in this case the leader was me. But before I could elevate, I needed to excavate. I had just been through a crushing personal business failure and my confidence was not just shaken; it had been destroyed.

I needed some therapy, and I got some, and as I did the homework my therapist assigned me, the healing began. As I wrote from my list of lessons under the working title, *Without Leadership Nothing Happens*, over time I began to realize that, although I had lost financially as a result of this failure, I had gained invaluable wisdom as a result of the hard lessons I had learned. That manuscript proved to be the best therapy, and although few will ever read it, it set me on this new path of *Pro Leadership.*

During my writing, my thinking changed in a subtle way; where I once thought like a Greek, I now found myself thinking like a Hebrew. Simply, the Greek way of looking at life is that failure is a disqualifier for leadership, while Hebrew thinking views failure as a necessary ingredient of success. The big lesson I learned is this: Our past is not prologue but preparation. In other words, if you fail, don't be afraid to start again; your experience qualifies you to lead.

Where I had once considered pro leadership to be a destination, I now see it as a journey, a journey where a leader establishes credibility, builds a following, and leads with impact.

Countless books have been written on leadership. I have read many and I'm sure you have too. After all, leaders are readers. This book is not meant to replace any of those; rather my hope is it will add to an already valuable library. In writing it, I had three goals:

1. to offer a fresh perspective on the vital role of leaders
2. to help readers change the way they think about leadership
3. to inspire, to equip, and to encourage leaders to "go pro"

Since *Pro Leadership* is not a destination, you won't arrive, unpack, and settle in. Rather, you are embarking on a journey, requiring you to saddle up and head out. With that in mind, ride on my friends!

1 | The Entrepreneurial DNA

"Most entrepreneurial ideas will sound crazy, stupid and uneconomic, and then they'll turn out to be right."
—Reed Hastings

> **PRO LEADERSHIP PRINCIPLE:** Entrepreneurial leadership thrives with freedom, authority, goals, and responsibilities.

I've never been able to drive by a kid with a lemonade stand without stopping. I have a practice of always supporting a budding entrepreneur—maybe because, once upon a time, the kid with the lemonade stand was me.

I was born and raised in Minneapolis, near the chain of lakes: Harriet, Calhoun, Isles, and Cedar. It was a great place to be a kid, and a great time to grow up. One Sunday afternoon each month, the park board would close one of the lakes to cars so bikers could enjoy the road. To me, even at ten years of age, it was a business opportunity.

I grew up in a home of modest means where my parents did not believe in an allowance. If I wanted something outside of what was needed, I had to earn the money myself. So, four hours with a guaranteed flow of customers who would be thirsty and hungry as a result of biking around a three-mile lake on a hot summer day presented a great opportunity. I seized it, loaded a table and a chair onto my wagon, hauled them a block and half down to the corner, and set up shop.

Of course, I had competitors (one quick ride around the lake proved it), but I was different. They had one beverage choice; I had three. They were Lemonade or Kool-Aid only; I had donuts. The first Sunday, after expenses, I made twenty bucks—not bad for a ten-year-old. In 1971, that was real money!

The entrepreneurial seed grew from there. When I was tall enough and strong enough to push the lawn mower on a flat surface, I began to help my dad with lawn maintenance. Soon, I could handle the front bank, and then the day came when the lawn officially became my responsibility. My dad trained me well—so well that five of our neighbors hired me to care for their lawns, and, as a result, I had my first business at the age of thirteen. Five lawns, mowed and trimmed weekly. It was fun, and I loved it. Plus, I had a pocketful of cash, and that meant I had freedom. It was a great feeling, one that has motivated me to recognize my entrepreneurial DNA and pursue it throughout my career.

Like my dad, most of my buddies' dads had good solid jobs. They worked hard, but they worked for someone else, and I would often hear complaints about "the boss." However, the parents of two of my closest friends never complained about "the boss"; they *were* the boss. It was from these two buddies I first heard the term "entrepreneur."

"Who does your dad work for?"

"He works for himself. He is an entrepreneur, and he produces and promotes entertainment."

(Wow, he's like me. He has his own "lemonade stand.")

Yes, these two dads were often at the office on Saturday, and once in a while, even Sunday, but they had other freedoms that most of the other dads in my life didn't have: they took us to mid-week baseball games, or pulled us waterskiing in the middle of the week because it was less crowded. Both had entrepreneurial DNA. One was a natural; the other learned the art of it and strengthened those muscles.

Strengthening the Entrepreneurial DNA

As I worked my way through college, I had multiple jobs, but they always ended up being replaced by some independent entrepreneurial endeavor that gave me control. I was a grinder at the Hopkins Iron Works; when a strike closed the company down and I could not work, I started a landscape business.

When I found out about the strike, I got into my car and drove to the local printer. I took a white sheet of paper, a black marker, and wrote: "College student needs work to pay tuition, will do any and all landscape work or other odd jobs—$10/hr." I added my phone number and had the printer make me 250 copies. That afternoon, I put them in mail boxes within a three-mile radius of my home. The next day, my phone started ringing, and for the next three summers, while I finished college, I had more work than I had hours to do it. Andrew Wyatt Enterprises paid for college. It also made me unemployable.

After I graduated from college, my first job was selling PCs as a corporate sales associate for Entre Computer Systems, and later for Amerisource. Both were value-added resellers, born from IBM, and owned and run by former IBM sales associates. There, I was given responsibility for a territory. Later, as

I succeeded, my responsibility increased and, along with it, my authority to build that territory.

Sales, we were taught, was a numbers game; the more numbers you did, the greater your sales. I found that to be true. In my first three months in my territory, I knocked on 1,000 doors. I was turned away by 90 percent of those, but the sales I made to the 10 percent who said "yes" made me the top producer in our branch. But it wasn't only the numbers that made me successful— it was the freedom and authority I had to make a deal, so I could achieve my sales goals and fulfill my responsibilities.

At the beginning of this chapter, I identified the first Pro Leadership principle: Entrepreneurial leadership is most successful when there is freedom and authority to accomplish goals and fulfill responsibilities. This lesson played out again as I journeyed in my career into the asset management business. A year as a straight-commission salesman taught me I didn't want to spend the rest of my career starting at zero on the first of every month. However, I wouldn't have been hired at my next job, Investment Advisers Inc., without the success I had selling computers. The CEO of IAI had grown up in sales, and he had been a sales manager. He believed you could teach everything but selling—he wanted "naturals." And that is what he said he saw in me. So, from corporate computer sales I moved to selling asset management services to wealthy individuals and their companies.

The CEO handed me a list of privately held companies in the five-state area: Minnesota, North Dakota, South Dakota, Iowa, and Wisconsin. "Call them all," he told me, and I did. Once again in my career, I was given freedom and authority to fulfill my responsibility and accomplish my goals. This led to the creation of a separate division at IAI we named the

Midwest Region. With over one billion dollars in assets, it was clearly a success. But with success came struggles, and soon, the company became the priority over our clients, and I no longer had the authority to fulfill my responsibility. In that circumstance, success became impossible and failure was guaranteed. Why? Because of the Pro Leadership principle we are discussing here: **that entrepreneurial DNA is most successful when there is the freedom and authority necessary to accomplish goals and fulfill responsibility.**

Ten years in the business world had taught me a lot, and with my entrepreneurial DNA, it wasn't surprising that it came time for me to follow my dream: to build a company. *Why not?* I reasoned. I would rather try and fail than get to the end of my life and wonder, *What if?* So, on November 1, 1993, I founded Cornerstone Capital Management, Inc. I now had the responsibility I had always wanted, and the freedom and authority to execute on our business plan and build a strong team. What did the entrepreneurial DNA accomplish? For the next twenty-plus years, my team and I built Cornerstone together. Sometimes we won and sometimes we lost, some decisions were right and some decisions were wrong, but we always endeavored to operate in the principles of leveraging freedom and authority to achieve goals and fulfill responsibilities.

As the leader, I made sure I always had (and used) the freedom and authority to act decisively, and we made sure all my associates had the freedom and authority they needed to succeed in achieving their goals and fulfilling their given responsibilities. The Cornerstone culture was entrepreneurial; we all won together and we would all lose together, but each team member could take ownership and pride in his or her contribution to our success, because they were all given what they needed to win.

Twenty-four years later, what started at zero had grown to over fifteen billion dollars in assets under management. What started in a basement grew to two thriving offices, one in Minneapolis and one in New York City. Two employees grew to sixty-five associates, composed of three investment teams and a trading operation. Building that firm and developing its leaders was one of the most fulfilling endeavors of my life. The majority of the building would not have happened had I not possessed well-developed entrepreneurial DNA.

A few years ago, I ran into my former boss and mentor, the CEO who hired me after I lost my computer sales job. I thanked him for all he had done for me, and told him I would never have built this business if I had not worked for him.

"How much are you managing?" he asked.

I responded, "A little over fifteen billion dollars."

"Good start," he said with a smile, then turned and walked away. Twenty-five years my senior and close to eighty, he could still fire me up. He was a pro leader.

Hallmarks of the Entrepreneurial DNA

When I think about what Pro Leadership requires, entrepreneurial DNA is a critical ingredient. In fact it is a hallmark of Pro Leadership, and if you desire to "go pro" you must develop it.

I believe the underlying driver of entrepreneurial DNA is a desire for freedom and the opportunity to create something bigger than yourself. Entrepreneurial DNA is just that simple: it is the desire to create. This desire expresses itself in various ways, one of those being the need for freedom.

Freedom is one of my governing values. I naturally seek it in all areas of my life. But what if you are not a natural creative with well-developed entrepreneurial DNA? I believe, as created beings, the seeds of it are within all of us, and to develop them and grow them takes only desire, the right environment, and time.

First of all, for that to happen, the environment needs to be entrepreneurial as opposed to institutional. An institutional environment where policies and procedures are paramount and do not allow for creativity to be expressed is an environment where freedom is limited and entrepreneurial leadership cannot grow. Institutional CEOs and the resulting infrastructures tend to lack the freedom and the authority to lead people and empower them in a creative way. These people and systems are often limited by the past and a corporate philosophy that is risk-averse as opposed to growth-oriented. They tend to be "historians," desiring to protect the past from the future. On the other hand, the entrepreneurial CEO is a "futurist"—learning from the past, but looking to the future and what can be created to meet it. It is a different mindset. It is offensive, not defensive.

So, how can you recognize entrepreneurial DNA, identify what characterizes it, and be intentional about developing these characteristics as you grow in your leadership? Entrepreneurial DNA is characterized by many things, some of the most recognizable being:

1. **Low risk aversion.** Low risk aversion is not being afraid to fail. It is not needing the security that comes with a salary. I have failed more times than I have succeeded. Failure is part of life, and the ability to accept it and to not be limited by it is a characteristic of entrepreneurial DNA.

2. **Vision-driven.** Every great endeavor begins with a vision. A vision is the jumping off point of any creative endeavor. People who have entrepreneurial DNA are vision driven. They see what can be before it is.

3. **High independence.** High independence is the characteristic that expresses itself in a strong desire for freedom. People who demonstrate this characteristic are effective working independently and, as leaders, allow others to work independently, too.

4. **Strong self-leadership.** Strong self-leadership is another common characteristic of the entrepreneurial DNA. John Maxwell, the great leadership influencer, says everything rises and falls on leadership, and the most important person a leader leads is himself or herself. As a leader, no one will tell you what to do or when to do it; you must be self-directed and self-disciplined to act on what is important *now*.

5. **Ability to ignore the crowd.** Every leader who has built something knows there will be opposition. If you are to succeed, you must be able to ignore the crowd—not only those who oppose you, but also those who believe in you. I used to believe it was only necessary to ignore the naysayers, but experience has taught me that even my supporters can become a distraction. I have learned to treat all comments, both discouraging and encouraging, as perfume. *(Smell it, don't swallow it.)*

6. **Perseverance.** There are very few overnight successes. Most stories of great leaders are ones filled with lessons of perseverance. Great leaders play through adversity, all the way to the end.

These are only some of the characteristics of entrepreneurial DNA. If you recognize them either in others or yourself, you will know you have encountered it. But what should you do if you do not see these characteristics in yourself? You need to cultivate them. I believe we all have within us these entrepreneurial muscles that can be developed and strengthened.

Exercising your entrepreneurial muscles will allow you to operate with the freedom and authority necessary to accomplish goals and fulfill the responsibilities required of a leader. In addition, you will not only become comfortable operating in this freedom and authority but you will be comfortable granting it to the leaders you are developing around you.

Principle Application

1. Do you naturally possess "entrepreneurial DNA," or is it a quality you will need to intentionally cultivate?

2. How have you experienced either the presence or lack of entrepreneurial DNA in your career up to this point?

3. Is there a story or principle from this chapter that inspired you, or provoked a thought about how you can stimulate and/or strengthen your own inner entrepreneur? Summarize it here.

2 | A Foundation for Leadership

"Leadership is about vision and responsibility, not power."
—Seth Berkley

PRO LEADERSHIP PRINCIPLE: (My strength) x (My Passion) = My Level of Fulfillment

---

Although I founded and was the CEO of an investment firm that grew to over fifteen billion dollars in assets under management, I had not made an investment decision in nearly 10 years. Our portfolio managers and analysts had that responsibility as a part of their roles. My primary role was leader, and my primary responsibility was to develop the leadership skills of my team.

Had I known what skills would be required to fulfill this role and responsibility, I would have picked a different major in college. Rather than majoring in Ag-Econ, I would have majored in Psychology! Building people requires different skills than building a portfolio, and I quickly learned that if you could not develop the right team, you would not succeed in building a winning, long-term investment record.

Of my twenty-four years in leadership, the last ten were spent entirely on building the people more than the company:

my associates, our clients, their consultants, and prospective clients. Over time, that focus became my passion.

This vision and calling did not come overnight; rather, it came over the course of time. And, to be honest, it was a skill I had to grow in. At, times I grew anxious about my future, and I had to learn a different response than the one that comes naturally to me. Formerly, my tendency would be to "take the bull by the horns" and "make it happen." My motto was, "If it is to be, it is up to me." I was a professional striver.

Yet, as I came to reflect on my many years of business experience, I realized my striving had, more often than not, resulted in an outcome that was less than the best. So, I decided to take a different tack. Whenever I became aware I was falling back into my habit of striving, I would stop and do the opposite. Rather than muscling my way through, I would pause, I would wait, I would write, I would pray, I would trust Providence to direct my path. This self-examination allowed many of my anxious moments to be replaced by peace. This peace is difficult for me to explain or even to write about. It is a mystery I do not fully understand, but someday I believe I will.

Leadership from a Place of Strength

Coaching and speaking to leaders on leadership fulfills me like nothing else—it is my passion. I have also come to learn, it is my strength. I learned something poignant about this from John Ramstead, a former Navy fighter pilot and leadership coach; that this is the formula for a fulfilled life—*the degree to which I am operating in my strength, multiplied by the degree to which I am operating in my passion, equals my level of fulfillment.*

(My strength) x (My Passion) = My Level of Fulfillment

It works like this: on a scale of one to ten, to what degree are *you* operating in *your* strength? Now, using the same measurement, to what degree are you operating in your passion? I have never seen two "tens," but I have seen leaders who had numbers that were eight or higher—that is my goal. On a scale of one to ten, I very rarely give a ten, which leaves no room for improvement. But Andrew Wyatt Leadership, LLC has resulted in my being at "eighty-one" on the fulfillment scale: nine for strength times nine for passion!

Try this exercise as a proof source: think back to an endeavor in which you did not feel fulfilled, and score it for strength and passion. I did it, and found I was less than sixty-four (eight times eight) in all of the endeavors that ultimately sucked the life out of me. Now, apply the exercise to what you are currently doing. Then answer this question for yourself: if sixty-four is your bar, where are you now? If you are below the bar, what are you going to do about it?

Clearing the Fulfillment Bar

When I coach one-on-one, my ultimate goal is to help my clients to clear the bar, the bar they alone can set. This is part of my coaching process, "the blueprint for leadership," and it has three phases: base camp, climb, and summit.

The base camp phase is knowing who you are, how you were made, and how you work. It is based on the principle of in before out. You cannot be effective on the outside until you are clear about what's inside.

The climbing phase is understanding your mission, what it means, and what it will require to fulfill it. In this phase you take what you know from the inside and plan its application on the outside.

The summit is the place where you know who you are, you are clear about your call, and you are clear about the strategy and the tactics necessary to fulfill your mission, and as a result you begin to live your life to the fullest.

Each phase is composed of a number of critical steps; each must be accomplished before moving on to the next. To skip any of the steps is to risk not only delay, but also a change in your destination. Each section of the climb will answer a number of questions, and, like building blocks, the answers you give will become the foundation for your success.

In base camp, you will answer five questions: who am I, what are my governing values, what are my roles, what is my why, and what is my calling? The purpose of answering these questions is, as I wrote above, to learn *who* you are, *how* you were made, and *how* you work. This is a tough phase because it requires a great deal of self-reflection, which may be difficult for some people, just as it was for me. So why do the work? Because no one can change the outside unless they are willing to either accept or change the inside. When answering the five base camp questions, here is how to frame your answers:

Question #1—Who am I? It all starts by answering this question. I am asking you to step in front of the mirror and take a good look into yourself. Ask anyone you see, "Who are you?" and the answer you will get from most people is what they do, not who they are. None of us are what we do; we are all more valuable than that. Who we are may determine what we do, but what we do is not who we are.

Question #2—What are my governing values? Think of these as the cylinders of your engine. They are your underlying motivation in all you do. They are the framework of your life. Values form as you grow, and they strengthen as you mature. They are the foundation you build your life upon. Values are not beliefs, because beliefs can change but values rarely do. As an example, I have seven governing values, these seven have not changed in the thirty years since I defined them, but I have clarified them over time. They are: faithfulness, generosity, leadership, excellence, simplicity, health, and freedom. For each of my values, I have written a clarifying statement. I won't share those because for the same value, your clarifying statement may be different. What matters is that for each of your values you have a specific clarifying statement.

Question #3—What are my roles? You will answer this by looking at your responsibilities and then tracing them back to the key people they are related to. For example, I have four roles: Husband, Father, Head Coach/Managing Partner, Friend. Just as I have a clarifying statement for each governing value, I have one for each role. You should have one for each role, too.

Question #4—What is my why? What juices you, what inspires you, why do you do what you do? I ask all of my prospective coaching clients to read Simon Sinek's *Start with Why*. If you don't have time to read the book or to listen to it on Audible, go to YouTube and find Sinek's Ted Talk, "Start with Why." We all have a why and discovering it will help you to clarify your direction and free you to move there (more on this in Chapter 4).

Once you have more clarity on what fulfills you and what your governing values are, and you are clear on your roles and your why, it will be easier to recognize the answer to question #5, *What is my calling*? Given all you know about yourself, what do you feel led to do? I like the question Robert Schuller asked John Maxwell, "What would you do if you knew you wouldn't fail?" Answering this question helped me to ultimately identify my call, and I have used it to help others to identify theirs, too.

Stick to Your True Calling—Then Keep Climbing

There are many benefits to answering the base camp questions. But, if I were to pick the best one, it would be that the answers to these questions will provide a foundation that will prevent you from being distracted from your true calling. Why? Because when the inevitable interruptions and distractions common to this life come along, your answers to these base camp questions will serve as a "true north" for you, always bringing you back on course toward your ultimate destination.

This is especially important as you continue in the climbing phase of leadership. In this phase, your vision is clarified, and you identify your aim and your aspirations. This results in a clear mission. I don't mean a mission that you simply carve onto a plaque that hangs in your office, but one that becomes a part of your life, a mission that you not only work for, but it works for you.

I am a vision-driven person; I need one to succeed and I believe you do, too. First comes your vision, the big dream for the future of your life, your vocation, and your business. Often times people are uncomfortable with vision; this is commonly the result of being risk averse, not wanting to believe something that may seem improbable. One of my favorite exercises as a coach is to help a client move into a visioneering state. It is simple and it is fun; it is also good for you. Here is how it's done.

The first step is to turn on your imagination. That's right, I said turn on your imagination, because adult life and the responsibilities and pressure of it will often cause that switch to be turned off. Think back to childhood; did you have any problem imagining yourself as anything? I doubt you did. What happened between then and now? Life happened.

So, take a break from life and dream a dream; see yourself as the leader you want to be and see your company where you want to lead it. Now, write it down. *Voila,* you have a vision! Let it "cook" for a while and see where it goes (i.e., let it settle in your thinking and allow it to help shape your direction and decisions). Remember the guiding question, "What would you do if you knew you couldn't fail?"

Next question: what is the aim of your vision? If it were fulfilled, where would this vision take you? Keep it simple.

I have seven aims and they are all "Be" statements: one is Be an Author—write five books. You are reading the first one right now. My aims have been revised and refined over time as my vision has grown or been fulfilled. Yours will too, so do not worry about being perfect, write down what comes to mind.

From your aim you go to your aspirations: why do you want to go where your vision will take you? This may be one thing or a list of things. I have found these to be bigger and broader desires—life-changing desires. You may not share these with many people outside of your inner circle, so don't worry about what "others may think" about what you aspire to. I am a possibility thinker who believes any aspiration a person has, given the talent, the time, and the environment, is possible.

A word of clarity: our aspirations need to fit with our natural talents and abilities. As an example, I love to play golf and sometimes I will imagine I am playing The Masters. In reality, I will never play at that tournament because no matter how strong my aspiration is to do so, I am not talented enough to get there, so it will remain an imaginary exercise and not an aspiration I will work toward.

The last part of the climb phase is your mission. This will be a reflection of a central governing belief. Often your "why" will be born from this. You read my "why" at the beginning of the chapter. It came out of my primary governing belief: **Without leadership nothing happens; strong, caring, servant leaders are good leaders and good leaders produce good outcomes.** Once you have defined your belief, you are able to form your mission.

It is possible that your "why" is your mission. I have seen this to be the case for many entrepreneurs, myself included. Take a look at your "why" and ask, "Is this my mission?" If your answer is yes, you're done and ready to move on to the final phase: the summit.

The View from the Top

The summit is where you take all you have learned on the inside and you move it to the outside, by turning the first nine steps of your climb into action. You translate your vision into reality. This last phase has four steps: clarifying your strategy, defining your tactics, acting to WIN, and leading yourself TODAY.

First, clarify your strategy. What are the big blocks that need to be moved in order to accomplish your call? Spell it out: identify your specific goal and what it is going to take to get there. What will you do when? Big picture. Let me give you an example, following up on one of my aims, be an author and write five books. In my strategy statement, I have spelled out generally the type of books I will write to fulfill this aim. What I am going to do is here and now; how I am going to do it comes next.

Next, define the tactics you will use to accomplish your strategy. What is it going to take to win? What specific steps will you need to take to fulfill your aim and when will you need to take them? Here you map it out. You have your goals, now make your plan, and then you will start acting on that plan to WIN.

WIN stands for "What's Important Now." It is a way to set priorities. I do it annually, every four months, monthly, weekly, and daily. Working on what matters most is critical to accomplishing goals. Using WIN and breaking my plan into specific time periods allows me to do that successfully.

Finally, remember that today matters. John Maxwell wrote a great book by the same title, *Today Matters.* You will accomplish all you desire, one day at a time. The more you can train yourself to live in the moment, the easier it will be for you to lead the most important person who needs your leadership. You. Legendary golf teacher, Harvey Penick, taught that a golf tournament is won one shot at a time. That is not only true of golf, it is also true of business and of life—one day at a time, one shot at a time.

I take the first day of every year to plan my year. I divide my year into three four-month periods. I take the first day of each of those periods to plan that period. I take the first day of every month to plan that month. I take forty-five minutes every weekend to review and plan my week. I take fifteen minutes at the end of every day to plan tomorrow. Does that mean everything goes according to plan? Hardly. However, the more often I focus on WIN, the faster I move toward my ultimate destination.

If you follow this blueprint for leadership, in time you will end up operating not only in your strengths, but also in your passion—which is a great foundation for living a fulfilled life.

Principle Application

1. How do you answer the following about your strengths and passions?

   What are your strengths?

   What are you passionate about?

   On a scale of one to 10, to what degree are you operating in your strengths?

   Using the same measurement, to what degree are you operating in your passion areas?

2. Do you feel fulfilled in your life?

   Why or why not?

3. What would you do if you knew you wouldn't fail?

3 | Know Yourself

"I think self-awareness is probably the most impor-
tant thing towards being a champion."
—Billie Jean King

> **PRO LEADERSHIP PRINCIPLE:** Pro leaders
> understand archaeology must precede architecture.

I love golf—it's my favorite pastime. The game is such a challenge. It's a journey, but you never arrive. I can appreciate why
legendary golfer Bobby Jones said it's the only game that the
more you play it, the harder it gets.

My golf season ends when the temperature drops below
fifty degrees. When that happens, I take my practice inside for
the winter. I am goal oriented, so at the start of each year I set
a goal for my game and, for the season. One of the measuring sticks I use to judge my progress is my USGA handicap.
Five years ago, when I returned to the game after a twenty-
year hiatus, my handicap was thirty-six-plus. If you're not a
golfer, this number essentially describes golf purgatory, neither Heaven nor Hell, simply ongoing frustration. Thanks to a
great PGA teaching professional, Luke Benoit, and a whole lot

of practice, what was once a thirty-six-plus is now a seventeen and trending lower.

But even though I have cut my handicap in half, I'm not satisfied. Now I have a new goal—can I get there? Luke says yes, BUT, one thing needs to change, and it's a big thing. My natural swing is outside-in and to play at the next level, it needs to be inside-out.

What's the big deal you say? This is the big deal: muscle memory. Every time I picked up a club, my muscles said swing outside in. How do you change that? One day at a time, one swing at a time, practice, practice, practice—doing the right thing over and over again, retraining my muscles.

As so often is the case, sport imitates life. Over the last several years, I have been working on another significant change—to the swing of my life. This was a key change I needed to make if I was going to become all I was created to be. However, in order to make the change, I realized, I first had to know myself. I had to be able to objectively assess myself the way my golf coach helped me objectively assess my golf swing.

In the last chapter, I told you I was a professional striver. Striving is what happens when one is living life from the "outside in." I have learned that living this way gets you nowhere but tied up in knots. In the long run, you are more likely to end up on a therapist's couch than you are a winner's podium.

Because I did not truly know myself, I spent the majority of my adult life living from the "outside in," and it wasn't until I finally examined and grew to know myself, objectively, that my life was transformed and I began to live from the "inside out." That "swing change" did more for my life and leadership than any other single act. This is key to Pro

Leadership, a true principle. And of all places, it was proven to me on the golf course.

But, like my golf swing, my problem here is one of muscle memory. In my case, I have over fifty years of striving, so it is my natural go to; I don't even need to think about it. The opposite of striving is abiding; a peaceful place where you know who you are and what your life's purpose is. Leaders who have checked these boxes are able to lead at the next level, because they no longer have their eyes on themselves, which allows them to focus on others. This is true leadership.

The Process of Self-Discovery

If you are not there now, you might be asking, *How do you get there? How do you work on this life "swing change"?* The answer I found is simple, but it's not easy. You must work on it every day. You must start and end each day by remembering who you really are, that you are a uniquely created being with an individual design and a higher purpose.

When the first chapter of my vocational life ended in 2017, I treated the months following it as "half time." It was a time for me to assess all that had led me to this place, a time to consider adjustments that needed to be made so my second half would allow me to finish the game with the outcome I desired. I read many books seeking help in answering the biggest question I had ever faced: *Who am I?* Had I not taken this "time out" to find out, I am quite certain you would not be reading this book today.

Knowing yourself does not happen overnight. No, like any other relationship in life, it takes time and focus. It is not always pleasant; sometimes it is just plain hard work. But it is good work, and like the time you spend on any relationship, it will bear positive results. What I learned from taking the time to answer the question is that if you want to be a pro leader, you have to do the work; you have to start here. Pro Leadership is inside out.

When I went into my "locker room" at half time, I was not happy with the score. I was losing, and I knew if I was going to win, adjustments needed to be made to my game plan. But where to start? I knew what everyone else wanted, but I did not know what I wanted. Like my golf swing, my life was being lived from the outside in. Yet, in a strange dichotomy, I came to understand the source of my frustration was not others, but myself. My eyes were opened to how selfish my pursuits had become. I thought I had been a servant leader when in fact I was nothing but a selfish leader. Pro leadership does not operate from selfishness. I needed transformation.

Diagnosis, I am told, is 85 percent of the cure. It may be true, but changing a way of thinking, one that has guided nearly all of my life, wasn't easy. Quitting smoking was easier. Fortunately, I had some good tools to aid my discovery (which I will share with you shortly), and they helped in the process of transforming me from striver to abider, from outside in to inside out, from self-focused to others-focused, a process that never ends.

Learning A New Swing

As I mentioned in the last chapter, at the beginning of every week, I review my personal mission and vision statement. Doing so has a centering effect, helping me to focus and determine my WIN, "What's Important Now." The first page of the document I use to do this is entitled: "Who Am I?" Even though the format may differ from person to person, I know now that this is where all great leaders start.

My page begins with a personal statement, affirming that I have been created for a purpose, and it is my goal to live for that purpose. Following that statement of affirmation, I have several other bullet points that together answer the question: *who am I?* It looks like this:

1. My Primary Identity—I have been created for a specific purpose and I have been given specific talents to use for the benefit of my fellow human beings.
2. On the Enneagram I am an 8 with a 7 wing—in growth I go to a 2 and under stress I go to a 5.
3. On the Myers Briggs type indicator, I am an INFJ—Introversion, Intuition, Feeling, Judging.
4. On Strengths Finder, my top five themes are: Relator, Responsibility, Activator, Maximizer, and Belief.

When I meet a leader for the first time, I like to ask him or her, "Who are you?" The majority of the time, they answer a different question, as if I'd asked, "What do you do?" Why? Because most people today do not know who they are; they only know what they do. It defines them. But the truth is, what we do is not who we are. Not knowing who you are is a sure sign you are living from the outside in. If that's you today, I know one thing about you; you are frustrated. You need a "swing change." You need to learn to live inside out.

For a while, until you have answered this question, you will need to turn your focus on yourself. Like I did, you too need to take a "time out to find out."

You might be asking, "Isn't this a self-focused, even selfish, exercise?" I don't think so. I believe it is the only way to know yourself, and to get to inside out living, which results in inside out leading, which is the foundation of all true servant leadership. It's how you go pro.

Assuming you agree, let's take the next step. You want to answer the question, *Who am I?* You want to learn and master a new swing. To do this, I want to teach you to use the three assessment tools I chose that helped me do just that. I want to tell you why I chose them and how I use them to inspire and equip leaders. My hope is they will inspire and equip you, too.

There are many tools to help anyone who desires to answer this question today; most are readily available online for a modest fee. I surveyed the whole landscape of resources, researched many, and settled on three: the Enneagram, the Myers Briggs type indicator, and Strengths Finder. Together, these assessments provided a three hundred and sixty-degree assessment of what makes me tick. By taking these evaluations and then studying the outcomes and the conclusions, I have been able to clearly answer that definitive question, *Who am I?*

Furthermore, by studying these three tools, I have come to have a greater sense for the strengths and weaknesses of each, coming to realize that alone they are not a panacea, but taken together, they answer 85 percent of the question. That 85 percent number is a principle I use in decision-making (see Chapter 17). I know I will rarely have *all* the answers, but if I can get 85 percent, I can make a good decision and, if necessary, gain the remaining 15 percent of what I need to know over time.

Strengths Finder

I started with *Strengths Finder 2.0*, Tom Rath's book defining 34 themes and ideas that were the result of Donald Clifton's work on Strength Psychology. Clifton's assessment reveals one's top five strengths. Rath explains them, the effect each strength has on you and others, and how you can put them into action in your life. My five strengths are:

1. Relator
2. Responsibility
3. Activator
4. Maximizer
5. Belief

This was a great place for me to start, and has proved helpful as I walk other leaders through this process. If you've never done it, I encourage you to go to www.gallupstrengthscenter. com and take the assessment. It's fun—and enlightening.

I took it when it first came out, and so did my wife and kids. It made for some lively dinner table conversation and led to a greater understanding of everyone at the table. It was so helpful in the inter-relationships of our family that I decided to use it in my business. Understanding my own natural strengths as well as those of my leadership team would help me to be a better leader. I ordered copies for all of my associates.

First, my leadership team took the test, and we plotted our outcomes on a chart to see how we fit together. Next, we plotted the strengths of all of our associates together, so we could understand both the strengths and weaknesses of the firm as a whole. The results led to a greater understanding of the unique strengths of each one of my associates. This allowed us to tailor our leadership to those we were responsible to lead.

I have taken the assessment three times, first with my family, next with my leaders, and finally when I took my "time out to find out." Interestingly, my results did not change over a ten-year period, the only difference was the order of the five. This I believe to be a result of maturation, and my guess is this would be true for most others as well. But the fact that my top five strengths did not change between 2008 and 2017 was enough proof for me that Strengths Finder is a reliable tool. It works, so I not only use it when I coach, I recommend it to anyone who is interested in answering the question, *Who am I?*

As an aside, if the Strengths Finder assessment is all you do, and if you read and think about Rath's definitions and action steps, you will have taken a big step in knowing yourself.

Myers Briggs Type Indicator

For me, the Strengths Finder assessment was not enough; I wanted to know *why* those five were my strengths. So, I took another step.

My second tool, the Myers Briggs type indicator (MBTI), took me deeper into understanding who I am. At my wife's urging, I took the MBTI assessment early in our marriage. She is a relational genius, keenly interested in what makes people tick. She is a knower and a lover of people. When I met her, she was on her way to a master's degree in Psychology. Although kids happened along the way, causing her to put her degree on hold, she never stopped studying, and I became her main client. She has been "shrinking" me for over thirty years.

During my half-time season, I took the assessment again, but this time, I did the study to understand what the results meant. On the Myers Briggs type indicator, I am an INFJ—my personality leans toward Introversion, Intuition, Feeling, and Judging. (You may find the assessment at www.myersbriggs.org.)

The MBTI is based on the work of Swiss physician Carl Jung and his book, *Psychological Types*, written in 1920. Isabel Myers and her mother, Kathryn Briggs, developed the MBTI and published it in 1962. It classifies sixteen personality types, one of which drives every individual. David Keirsey, in his book, *Please Understand Me II*, further developed and defined the 16 personality types, making it easier to learn and to understand the effect your natural type has on your life and on others.

Basically, the assessment measures your personality on four continuums:

1. Introversion versus extroversion
2. Sensing versus intuition
3. Feeling versus thinking
4. Perceiving versus judging

The combination of your tendencies will put you into one of the sixteen different categories, which even in themselves can vary, based on the degree to which you characterize the various tendencies. This understanding has had a significant impact on my leadership and my ability to answer the question, *Who am I?*

It also helps me understand, *Who are YOU?* Once you learn the basics of the assessment process, you can often quickly assess the (basic) personality of another person. This can help bridge the gap of understanding that invariably happens when we relate to other humans (i.e., "real life"). If we can understand other people's needs and motivations, and we are self-aware of our own, much miscommunication and misunderstanding can be eliminated without saying a word!

If you have never taken the MBTI, I hope you'll do it. In fact, it can help you to understand yourself—why and how you do what you do—as well as the people around you. At the very least, it will help lead the most important person you lead each day, yourself.

The Enneagram

The third leg of my "who am I" stool was the Enneagram, an ancient personality map that divides personality into nine types. Each individual has three variations of type, which results in twenty-seven pathways to personality. Although it sounds complicated, it is not, and it is remarkably accurate.

Taking the ancient assessment, and studying my results, has given me a greater self-awareness than any other personal assessment. On the Enneagram, I am an "8" with a "7 wing." In growth, I go to a "2" and under stress I go to a "5." That probably sounds like gibberish to you, so you'll just have to believe me when I say it really does make sense when you get into it! If you are so inclined, you can start by taking the assessment at www.enneagraminstitute.com and then take a look at one of Beatrice Chestnut, PhD's books, either *The Complete Enneagram*, or *The 9 Types of Leadership*. When I was first introduced to it, I was a skeptic, but the more I studied the Enneagram, the more I realized it was an outstanding complement to the MBTI and Strengths Finder. Taken together, they offered me a remarkably accurate three hundred and sixty-degree assessment of who I am.

I have to say, that another advantage to the self-awareness that comes as a result of being able to answer for yourself, *Who am I?* is that, by knowing who you are, you will consequently know who you're *not*. This knowledge will embolden your confidence and decision-making, because you will recognize what you are made for and what you're not. Granted, this requires a healthy dose of humility. However, it's worth it. You will be better able to lead yourself and, as a result, you will be a better leader all around.

A final thought on these assessment tools. None judge which personality traits are best; rather, they are meant to be descriptive in nature. No one is judged good or bad based on the results of any of these assessments.

Humility in Self-Awareness

It's virtually impossible to have an authentic conversation about self-discovery and self-awareness without also discussing the topic (and urgent need for) humility. Humility is one of those qualities that can be extremely painful to gain, but is immensely valuable once you obtain it, if you are willing to embrace it.

Humility gets a bad rap today. It shouldn't, but it does, because in our social media-saturated society where our focus is increasingly on self-promotion, many people fear that if they are humble, no one will notice them. If this statement sounds true to you, and you feel you need social media to be heard or validated, then you are living from the outside in. You are likely not being your most authentic self. If that is the case, that will need to change if you are going to be a pro leader.

True humility, though some might perceive it as weakness, is actually a strength—and a key ingredient in all great leaders. To better understand it, let's start with a proper working definition of it.

Humility is not thinking less of yourself, it is thinking of yourself less. But, you say, "I need to think about myself!" Yes, you do, but do it honestly. See yourself as you truly are, with both weaknesses and strengths. Humility is admitting weaknesses and then moving on and applying your strengths.

I am both good and bad; my life is a tension between the two that I must manage. I heard Billy Graham interviewed and he was asked about humility. I cannot recall the specific question, but I will never forget his answer, "We all have two dogs in us, fighting all the time—a good dog and a bad dog. The one that wins is the one you feed the most."

I am not a naturally humble person; in fact, when I speak publicly of my personal journey, my first words are usually, "I was arrogant and prideful." Hubris would not be an inappropriate descriptor. I hesitate to say I am humble even today, but I will say, I have been humbled, and as I look back, no one needed it more. What I learned is that arrogance, pride, and the hubris that results from those, comprise the opposite side of the coin, which is insecurity. It wasn't until I came to that understanding that I became okay with humility and was able to be honest with myself and others.

In the chapters that follow, we will return to this theme of strengths and weaknesses, admitting your own and building a team where together you complete and balance each other. But for here and now, this is a good place for you to take your own "time out" to answer a few self-evaluation questions. These are four questions I have adapted from a book by Jay Coughlin, *Tru Balance*, thinking about the question, *Who am I?* Answer these for yourself:

- What are the good things about me?
- What would I like to change about myself?
- How can I minimize the impact of my weaknesses?
- How can I maximize the impact of my strengths?

Were you able to answer these honestly? Well done! Knowing yourself is critical to establishing your credibility, not only with others but with yourself. Doing so lays a cornerstone in the foundation of Pro Leadership, which, if done honestly, thoughtfully, and with humility, will last for the rest of your life.

Now there is one more step in our process of excavating before we elevate. It is answering the second of the two big questions: what's your why? This is your driving motivation for doing what you do. This will be work, just as knowing yourself was work, but it will be fun work, and in the end very profitable. When I coach leaders, we always start with "knowing yourself," just as you have done here, because only then will you be able to uncover your "why." Doing that will be transformational to you and those you lead.

Get ready to have some fun in the next chapter!

Principle Application

1. On a scale of one to ten, where do you think you land in the area of self-awareness?

2. How would you answer the question, "Who are you?" as opposed to the more common, "What do you do?"

3. Toward the end of this chapter, you read the following self-assessment questions. Take some time and space here to answer them now:

   • What are the good things about me?

- What would I like change about myself?

- How can I minimize the impact of my weaknesses?

- How can I maximize the impact of my strengths?

4 | What's Your Why?

"If you lose your way, you have forgotten your why."
—George Grant

> **PRO LEADERSHIP PRINCIPLE:** People who know how follow people who know why.

I love history—specifically about great leaders. I believe Winston Churchill was correct when he said that history is the study of the lives of those people who made it.

My favorite leaders to study are American Presidents. I want to know how they made decisions, especially the tough ones. I am working my way through them all, and, so far, I have read extensively about Washington, John Adams, Jefferson, Jackson, Lincoln, Teddy and Franklin Roosevelt, Truman, Eisenhower, Reagan, and the Bushes. In addition to these, I have added the other Founding Fathers—those great early entrepreneurs without whom you most likely would not be reading this book. I've also read and studied the lives of Winston Churchill and Nelson Mandela; both are on my "hero list."

One common thread I see running through all of the lives of these great leaders is the ability to make tough decisions; in fact, those decisions defined their greatness. Their decisions were rarely black and white, rather, different shades of gray. The pro/con factor of each decision was often unclear. Yet, time was always of the essence, so delaying the decision was not an option. All of these leaders had strong counsel, but in the end, all were left alone to make the decision, and they had the courage and the conviction to make it. They all were pro leaders.

When it comes right down to it, a leader's primary responsibility is decision making. Sometimes you are right and sometimes you are wrong, but you must always act. So, here's a question for you—when leadership requires you to make a decision, have you ever:

- Wondered what to do?
- Wrestled with it?
- Said "yes" when, in your heart, you knew you should have said "no"?

If you answered "yes" to any of the above questions, you are not alone. How then, is a "good" decision made?

Finding Your Inner Motivation

When a pro leader makes a decision, he or she has to start with the "why." This is a foundational principle of leadership: people who know *how* follow those who know *why*. Leaders must know their why. No one will be a good and effective leader unless they do. If you desire to go pro in your leadership, you too must know your why.

You may be leading without a clear why as you read this, and you may have been doing so for some time, but now you are realizing your need to define it. On the other hand, you may have already identified your why; if so, what follows will only affirm how important it is to your leadership. In any case, it may be helpful for you to take a break and watch Simon Sinek's Ted Talk on starting with why:

https://www.ted.com/talks/simon_sinek_how _great_leaders_inspire_action

In my practice, before I begin a one-on-one coaching relationship, I ask my client to watch Sinek's Ted Talk and to read his book, *Start with Why*. My own leadership improved immensely by both the talk and the book. To me, it wasn't necessarily new information that I gleaned from them, but rather a positive perspective and a clarifying framework which allowed my why to become a useful leadership tool for myself and others. My own personal why is: *"to inspire and equip leaders who desire to develop the leader within and to become all they were created to be."* Clarifying my why has done more to help me in decision-making than any other single thing.

If you have read this far, I am confident that you are a leader who desires to develop the leader within. You realize you have entrepreneurial DNA, which you desire to grow and strengthen; you have acknowledged the need for a blueprint for leadership, and you have taken a time out to know yourself. You are well on your way to establishing your credibility—the first step in pro leadership. Now you are ready to answer the biggest and most important question, "What's my why?" It's my desire to guide you to your answer, but it must be your answer, no one else's will do.

The greatest leaders I have ever studied—who were all, I might add, in the category of "servant leaders"—were crystal clear on their why. This is a critical ingredient to this style of leadership. You cannot have true servant leadership without knowing your why, because it is what motivates and energizes you. A true why helps you get out of bed each morning, and enables you to serve the people you lead. In enables you to focus on the bigger picture, and allows you to put their needs before your wants when necessary.

In my coaching experience, I've observed that most people have their why deep within themselves already, and it only needs to be drawn out. Once uncovered, it will fuel your passion and lead to a fuller life and more impactful leadership experience. I've seen leaders get a dramatic "turbo charge" in their leadership transformation whenever they uncover their why. With that in mind, let's go for it!

The Importance of Knowing Why

The probability of making a good decision will go up exponentially if you know your why. It will also enable you to more easily determine what you shouldn't do. As a leader, you will be asked to do many things, and the truth is, you will need to say no much more often than you say yes. Knowing your why will help you clearly determine what fits and what doesn't, allowing for a quicker no and, as a result, more time to focus on your yes (and the right yeses at that).

Furthermore, once you have made the decision, and the going gets tough (as it always does), having made the decision to move forward based on your why will allow you to have both clarity and conviction in your decision. This will help you to carry out the decision with confidence, and to make any necessary course corrections during your journey. Think of your "why" as your compass, your north star; it will help you stay the course.

Finally, knowing why will make you a better leader. Remember, people who know *how* follow people who know *why*. Effective leadership requires you to influence others to follow you toward your articulated vision for your mission or organization. A clearly defined why will allow you to communicate this clearly with your people, which will result in their understanding of the why. This allows your influence to impact them and guide them toward your common goal.

How I Got to My Own Why

I had been giving a certain talk to business leaders and to students on college campuses for over ten years. At the time, I did not know why (actually, I did, but it hadn't been articulated yet). I needed circumstances and experience to draw out my purpose.

The title of the talk was "*Without Leadership, Nothing Happens.*" It was an inspirational talk, encompassing my life story with an emphasis on my business journey. Although the title had become my mantra, it took over a decade to evolve into my why. It wasn't until I was able to answer the question, "Who am I" that I could move on to identifying and fulfilling it.

My why is summed up in one sentence that answers two questions: 1) **to** (do what), 2) **so that** (this is the outcome). Again, I am indebted to Simon Sinek's work for drawing out my why. But I needed to take another step to validate it. A good why doesn't come cheap. If you get it right on the first "draft," you are unique. I know it took me a little over a month of multiple iterations for me to settle on it. Even then, it was only 85 percent correct. The next few months got me to 95 percent, and that's good enough, for now.

Again, my why is: *To inspire and equip leaders, who desire to develop the leader within, to become all they were created to be.* As I developed my why, I realized I had what I call a "governing belief" and it was this belief that birthed my why. Here's how I made the discovery: One day, I was talking to an entrepreneurial founder/CEO about leadership. As if on cue, he asked me about my "why." I recited my freshly minted "why" statement. I will be forever grateful for his next question: "Why?"

My answer was a knee-jerk one: "Without leadership, nothing happens." This led to a lengthy conversation about good and bad leadership, good and bad decisions, good and bad outcomes. This resulted in another personal "time-out" to seek out the root of my why. In the end, it was my core governing belief: without leadership nothing happens; strong, caring, servant leaders are good leaders, and good leaders produce good outcomes.

Now It's Your Turn

You can find your own why too; you only need to start where you are now. What is it that inspires you? What do you love to do? What would you do for free? At the beginning of my business career, my why was to become a millionaire—not a good why! And why not? Because that is an aspiration rather than a why. Aspirations, I have found, won't fuel me when the going gets tough. But a true "why" will.

With this in mind, I encourage you to write down your answers to the three questions above, then answer these questions for each: "Why does it energize you, why do you love it, and why would you do it for free?" Write down your answers. Then, turn over your page, so you have a new blank page. Write down the answer to this question: "If you knew you could not fail, what would you do?" And then, "Why would you do it?"

Next, put this page of questions in your pocket (virtually, not necessarily literally) and let it simmer for a few days. Don't forget about it. Think about your answers, meditate on them, edit and revise them.

This makes me think of my wife's soup. She makes the best soup I have ever tasted—always made from scratch and never in a hurry. The aroma fills our house for two days, then on the third day I ask, "What's for dinner?"

"Soup," she says.

Just as great soup needs time to simmer, so does a true why.

One other piece of advice: don't share your why, not yet. Keep it to yourself for a while. You are in the early "creative" stage, and you don't want comments or opinions from others. At this early stage, their feedback might distract you. Only you truly know yourself. Save yourself from outside comments until you get to the "testing" phase. At that point your why will be developed enough for it to stand up to unnecessary discouragement from others. Remember, your why is the fuel of your passion, not theirs.

Most leaders I have interviewed are not leading with their why. I find the 80:20 principle is true in this case: 80 percent of leaders are not leading from their why; only 20 percent of the leaders I have interviewed know and lead from a self-awareness of their inner motivation. This is another reason you must guard your why in its early stage. Yours will be unique, and therefore more vulnerable to criticism. Don't let in the opinions of others during this critical time of developing your why.

After it has been cooking for a few days, take another clean page from your notebook and do the above exercise again. Compare your answers. My guess is that they will have been refined. Like a good soup, time has created a chemical reaction that makes it "just right." At this point, you should be able to write one sentence that looks like this: To. . . , so that. . . . For example: **To** *grow in my leadership skills,* **so that** *I may help my team succeed.*

Now you are ready for the testing phase. This is the stage where you take your why public; you memorize it and look for "natural" opportunities to share it with others. You're not asking their opinion, because it's not relevant. They are not you. Rather, you are gauging natural reactions. This is the fun part (if you allow it to be) so enjoy it. At this point, your why is not carved in marble; you need a gut feeling about its accuracy. The best way I know to do that is to take it for a spin and see if it feels and sounds like you. If it does, you have validated your why and it will begin to influence you and what you do from this day forward. If it doesn't, simply repeat the first exercise.

At this stage in my own self-exploration, I was 70 to 85 percent of the way to my why. "Going public" got me to 95 percent. The reason I'm not at 100 percent is that I don't want my why to ever be off the table. I believe time and experience will refine and clarify it; it will evolve, and I want to leave room for that. Allow room for that to happen with your why, too.

The Power of Why

Since discovering my why, I can attribute the following list of benefits to living and leading from understanding my inner motivation. Knowing "why":

- will help you get out of bed in the morning
- helps you make good decisions
- helps you communicate with the people you lead
- helps you prioritize and know "What's Important Now" (WIN)
- saves time
- prevents anxiety
- prevents confusion
- creates confidence
- creates momentum
- gives balance
- is encouraging and inspiring
- provides calm
- is freeing
- will help you be all you were created to be

These are some, but not all of the benefits of knowing your why. I am sure that the list will grow for you as you live and lead from your own.

Before you move on, I encourage you to take some time to reflect on where you have been and on how far you have come. Give the recognition of your entrepreneurial DNA, your blueprint for leadership, and your recognition of your inner motivation time to "simmer" together.

Congratulations! You have now taken the first step in "going pro." You have established your credibility and laid a strong foundation on which to build your platform. Nicely done. The next step in Pro Leadership is building your following, and if you apply the wisdom found in the pages ahead, you will do just that.

―――――――― **Principle Application** ――――――――

1. Take some time to uncover and articulate your why. Start with these three questions. Then, below that, write out what you believe your "why" is.

   • What is it that inspires you?

   • What do you love to do?

   • What would you do for free?

   My why:

2. Can you identify your governing belief?

3. How do your why and your governing belief influence your leadership?

5 | It's All about Relationships

"Almost everything in leadership comes back to relationships."
—Mike Krzyzewski

> **PRO LEADERSHIP PRINCIPLE:** Leadership
> begins and ends with relationships.

For nearly five years, I commuted from Minneapolis to New York weekly. There are a lot of interesting things about working in a large city like New York, but one is the number of famous people who can be seen. In fact, I saw many famous people in New York, although I did not get to actually *meet* or interact with them.

Who is the most famous person you have ever met? I don't mean who is the most famous person you have seen, perhaps in a movie or in passing—I mean actually *met*? For me, the answer to this question is easy—my hero, Nelson Mandela. He had just finished his Presidency of South Africa and was on a tour of the United States. The tour included a day in Minneapolis, with a speech at the Minneapolis Club, the city's old-line business club. Space for the event was limited, but Mandela was a modern-day George Washington and a once-in-a-generation leader, so I quickly bought two tickets, one for me and one for my friend, Daniel Luthringshauser (who, before he retired, had lived in South Africa).

When we arrived, it was a mob scene of adoring people. People were awestruck and clamoring to see him! I did not expect anything other than to be in the same room with Mandela—simply to see him and hear his voice, live and in person. His speech was awesome. He was humble, gentle, and kind, but he was also resolute, and he exuded a confidence and a power I have only witnessed in others who, like him, have suffered greatly. He was poised. It was inspiring to be in the room with such a great man; even from a hundred feet away I had goose bumps!

When the program ended, we stood up from our table, which was in the back corner of the room, and Daniel turned to me and asked, "Would you like to meet Madiba?" I had read Mandela's autobiography and learned this was the name his friends called him. It is a term of endearment and respect.

"Absolutely," I replied, not anticipating what was going to happen.

"Okay, follow me," Daniel replied. What happened next will be one of those few things I expect to remember on my death bed. I followed Daniel across the room to where about a hundred people were standing around Mandela. We were about twenty feet away when Daniel caught his eye. Mandela turned, looked right at Daniel, smiled warmly, and said, "Daniel, my friend, what a pleasant surprise that I would see you today."

The crowd went quiet and parted to let Daniel through, and I followed right behind. The two men embraced like long lost brothers. Then Daniel said to him, "Madiba, I would like to introduce you to my good friend, Andy." I stuck out my hand and smiled, but I was speechless.

Nelson Mandela took my hand, looked me in the eye, and said, "Any friend of Daniel's is a friend of mine." Then, for the next ten minutes, as he spoke with Dan, he held my hand the entire time. Not since my own father did when I was a boy had anyone held my hand like that.

Wow. Nelson Mandela did not even know me. I was one of the least of all who were in attendance that day, but he made me feel like a king! I felt worthy and seen and respected. It was one of the finest relational gestures I have ever experienced, and I will never forget it.

Now I can say not only have I have *seen* and *met* Nelson Mandela, but also that I—at least on a limited scale—actually *knew* him, because we have interacted personally. My friend Daniel actually had a *relationship* with him.

This sliding scale of the degree of a relationship that I've just mentioned is important, because how we are able to navigate it, prioritize it, and leverage it will profoundly affect our pro leadership quotient. With that in mind, lets dive into the important topic of relationship building.

How Relationships Influence Leadership

Leadership guru John Maxwell often says, "Everything rises and falls on leadership." What makes it rise and fall is relationships. That is why I shared Duke basketball coach Mike Krzyzewski's words at the beginning of this chapter: "Almost everything in leadership comes back to relationships." The application of this principle of relationship is one of the major points that causes leaders to rise or to fall, to thrive or to languish, to succeed or to fail.

Relational skill is a common attribute of all great leaders. Nelson Mandela is named on every modern day list of great leaders that I have ever seen. The day I met him, I gained a clear insight into one aspect of his greatness; he is a master of relationships. Not many will attain his level of relational skill, but if you aspire to be a pro leader, and build a strong following, you will need to grow in this way.

As human beings, we are all uniquely emotional creatures, and as a result, we have within us the ability to relate emotionally to our fellow human beings on a pretty deep level. Your ability to do this well (relate to others emotionally) will directly affect your ability to influence your followers. If you are not a person of influence, you will not be an effective leader.

Abraham Lincoln said, "People don't care how much you know until they know how much you care." Caring is a critical ingredient of leadership. If your followers do not believe you care for them, they will not follow for long. A leader demonstrates care by connecting emotionally with followers. Some leaders never connect emotionally—only intellectually. When this happens, followers are equipped with knowledge, which motivates their following in the short term, but they are never inspired, so they don't follow the leader long term.

Relational skills fall into the category of Emotional Quotient (EQ). Distinct from intelligence (IQ), which is often fixed, EQ is a skill that may be developed and grown. While I have not experienced anyone growing their IQ, I have witnessed many refine and strengthen their EQ. Some are naturally high in EQ, but everyone has room to grow. Developing this relational muscle will do nothing but add richness to your life and your leadership.

Self-Assessment: How Good Are You at Building and Sustaining Relationships?

Connecting emotionally is an incredibly vital skill. I liken it to weight training: it is most effective when you work from a pre-determined workout routine or plan. The same is true in building your relational strength. You need to practice deliberately and consistently over time, sharpening your skill and learning as you go.

Since everything rises and falls with leadership, and almost everything in leadership comes back to relationships, we need some good metrics that will help us develop this skill. For an accurate self-assessment, as with any other skill, you will need to identify where you are in the process.

Start by making note of all of your relationships. Look back at the roles you identified in Chapter 2, "The Foundation for Leadership." Consider each role and list the individuals you relate to as you fulfill that role. Next, rate each relationship. Is it: strong, building, or needing work? A **strong** relationship is one in which you may be open and honest; it is a two-way street with mutual care, concern, and trust. A **building** relationship is just that: you are getting to know one another, and you are building trust and mutual respect. Think of a relationship that **needs work** like grass that has gone dormant in the winter, or due to lack of water. These types of relationships need attention and effort. Relationships go dormant for a host of reasons and only you can answer why, but you know it is one that will need some water, warmth, and sunlight before it greens up. (Everyone has relationships in each category, so don't fret if the "needs work" category tips the scale.)

I think of relationships as cyclical and perpetually in motion, but the motion is variable. For example, I have an old friend I met in the first grade. He lives on the other side of the world now and we rarely see each other. Thanks to FaceTime, our relationship is greener than it has been in years, but it is not the same as when we are together. Yet, because of our long history, it does not take much work to turn this relationship green again. It may be years since we have been together, but we often laugh that the first word of our conversation is, "Furthermore!" Relationships such as this move quickly back to strong and thriving. Others require effort and patience before they will green up (and that's okay). All this to say, don't judge yourself; rather, keep moving forward. I don't believe any relationship is beyond repair.

Many relationships in need of repair are with people of the past. My personality is that of a futurist, not a historian; I am not one who typically dwells on the past. That said, none of us can afford to ignore our relational pasts, so it is wise to take a moment and consider past relationships and how they played out. Life is both good and bad, so past relationships will fall into each column. Do not be afraid as you consider your role in past relationships. Remember, you are not judging, you are assessing so you may grow stronger.

Consider past relationships this way for now: *Did it give me life, or did it drain life from me?* Then answer, *Why?* When I have done this exercise, where I have become aware of a broken relationship due to my actions, I will make an effort to mend the fence. Here is where boundaries are so critical, because you can only control your own actions; you cannot control the responses of others. I will expand on boundaries at the end of this chapter.

As one moves down life's road, some past relations will be remembered fondly, but being human, others will be remembered painfully. Use both to help you learn and grow.

The final step in your assessment is planning how you will handle relationships in the future. This is not about others; it is about you deciding to build your relational muscles. No matter what your level of relational ability, you can grow it. Relational ability is an open system, like muscle, it can always grow. The only thing you need to get started is the desire and the commitment to do it.

Building Relational Muscle

You will need some tools to accomplish your goal. Your main tool will be your attitude. With the proper attitude, building relational muscle is a three-step process.

The first step is to establish **your position**. "Inside out," the posture/perspective I've mentioned before, is the proper soil in which to grow relationship. In Chapter 3, *Know Yourself,* you learned to identify who you are. You will not succeed long term in a relationship that does not honor who you are. Bringing your best to relationships requires bringing the authentic you into the relationship. Hence, you will want to work on your relationships from the inside out. I encourage you to make this your relational mantra: "I will bring my true self to every relationship." If this can be true for you, you will be building your relationships on a solid foundation.

As well, you will be applying your best efforts to the only person in a relationship that you can actually change, and that is yourself. So often, we expend our efforts trying to change other people, which is virtually impossible! But if we know ourselves, and can adjust our own attitudes and expectations based on what we know about ourselves and others, we can bring incredible health and strength to our relationships, and release others from our unhealthy expectations that *they* need to be the ones to change. It's amazing to see how our relationships with others fall into place more organically when we have been working on ourselves first.

Next is **your priority**—that is, to focus on your strengths. In Tom Rath's book, *Strengths Finder 2.0*, he makes the strong case for focusing on your strengths. Our strengths and weaknesses come with us into all relationships. Strong relations are built upon strengths—not weaknesses. I do not mean you should ignore your weaknesses; I mean, don't focus on them.

Think about it like this: I love to play golf and, of the three parts of the game (long game, short game, and putting), I am strongest with my short game, followed by putting. As a result, I spend 80 percent of my practice time at the short-game practice area and only 20 percent at the range working on my long game. I focus on my weakness just enough so, at worst, its effect on my score is neutral in a round. Work invested in my short game and putting pays the biggest dividends over a round. Strengthening my strengths is where I gain the most benefit. It works the same with relationships.

The last step in building relational muscle is keeping **your perspective,** by answering the question, "What type of relationship is this?" Again, your answer will relate to which role the relationship falls into. As an example, in my life, I have four primary roles: husband, father, head coach of Andrew Wyatt Leadership LLC, and associate/friend. Obviously, my roles as a husband and a father are very clearly defined by who I relate to in those roles. As I move out and my role expands, so do the number of people I relate to in those roles. It is critical to keep a relational perspective appropriate to each role.

Relationship does not always mean friendship, but it does always mean respect. No matter how strong your relational muscle, there will always be some people you just don't like. It's normal; you're human! On a personal note, I have learned that, many times, the people I "just don't like" are often just like me! As a result, conflict occurs between us, and I have learned conflict is a normal part of life. How you navigate that inevitable conflict makes all the difference in the world.

Four Tactics for Effective Relationship-Building

Now that we have established some strategies for building relationships, it is fitting to consider four tactics critical to accomplishing the goal. The first tactic relates to whom you will have relationship with and the last three are commitments you will make to each relationship: being present, being vulnerable, and having good boundaries.

1. **Start with the WHO.** I like to think of this as a relational map. Think of concentric circles. At the center is YOU. The closer the circle is to the center, the more vital the relationship.

   Each of your roles may represent a circle. Every leader needs an "inner circle." As you consider the relationships in your leadership following (including family, friends, work, etc.), start from the inside and move out. You will naturally have the most influence and impact the closer you are to your center.

In my coaching practice, when I am one-on-one with a client, I ask pointed questions about the quality of his or her personal relationships, beginning at the center and working out. In leadership as in life, the head follows the heart, so those relationships closest to the heart are the foundation. If you get those right, all else will more easily fall into place.

2. **Be present.** This is critical to building relationships and your following. You have likely heard the saying, "Absence makes the heart grow fonder." I have learned this is only a partial truth. Here is the whole truth: absence makes the heart grow fonder, unless you are absent too often, then they just forget about you! This common saying is generally referring to a physical absence. But what is critical to relationships is also to not allow *mental* absence when you are in another person's presence.

When I am in a coaching session, my goal is to be fully present. To have a singular focus on my client. To listen intently. For that session, my client is the only one who matters. I put everything outside of myself in "airplane mode." This action demonstrates to whomever I am with that they are my priority, and as a result our relationship is strengthened. This goes for my wife and children and anyone else that I'm in relationship with. I can't say that I always achieve it 100 percent of the time, but I have made it my goal.

My dad died long before the digital age, but this one lesson he taught me about building relationships has helped me more in this digital age than any other—to always be present with the person you are with. Every time you are with someone and you put your devices in "airplane mode," you say to them, "you matter." Everyone is inspired and encouraged by sensing and that their thoughts, their opinions, and their work matters to you. As John Maxwell says, "This is relational gold."

3. **Connect.** Again, John Maxwell says often that you cannot lead someone—you cannot win their mind—until you have first won their heart. To do that, you must be vulnerable. Generally, people will only be vulnerable with you to the degree you are vulnerable with them.

I learned this lesson many years ago when I was asked to speak to a large group of men. It was my first time speaking to a large group, so I was nervous. I reached out to a mentor of mine, who was an accomplished speaker, and asked his advice. "A good speaker connects with his audience," he said. "If you want to connect, you must be willing to be vulnerable, and if you aren't willing to do that, don't waste their time speaking." Then he hung up.

Here is what I heard: there is no room for ego on the podium. This is not only true of speaking and writing, but it is also true of relationships. So, check your ego at the door and open yourself to the other person; be vulnerable. I do not mean be indiscreet. It is possible to be vulnerable without being indiscreet. This is vulnerability appropriate to the person and the relationship you are addressing. For instance, as a leader there are some things you will discuss with your inner circle that would not be appropriate to discuss outside of it. Pro leadership understands the what level of vulnerability promotes connection and what level hinders it. Pro leaders want to avoid getting a text back afterwards—*TMI* (too much information)!

4. **Have healthy boundaries.** I have learned that healthy boundaries are one the most critical ingredients of strong relationships. I have never met a strong leader who did not have and understand good boundaries. Think of boundaries as you would a clear property line or a fence. It is not a wall keeping people out; rather, a boundary is a relational fence, telling everyone, *this is where you end and where I start.* As G.K. Chesterton wrote, "Don't ever take a fence down until you know the reason it was put up." Boundaries are so critical to pro leadership I recommend all my clients study the topic, and I hope you will too.

Of all I have studied on this issue, Henry Cloud's work is the most applicable. If you have not read *Boundaries* or *Boundaries for Leaders,* you owe it to yourself to do so. Make one of them the next book you read or listen to as you develop and refine your relational skills.

Starting today, I believe if you apply these four principles, you will build and strengthen your EQ and your relational following. Furthermore, if you continually assess your relational skills and if you make an effort to build relational muscle, I guarantee you, over time, your life will grow richer, and as a result you will gain confidence in your inner personal skills and influence.

But before we leave this vital topic, I want to give you some questions to reflect on as you build and maintain relationships—a little science behind the art. Whoever you relate to today, assess the relationship. Ask yourself:

- Which of my roles does this relationship fall into?
- What is the condition of this relationship?
- Does it need to change?
- If so, what action do I need to take?
- Am I being myself?
- Can I and do I bring my strengths to this relationship?
- Am I being present?
- Am I being vulnerable?
- How are my boundaries?
- Would this person say I care about them?

Getting your arms around the importance of relationships is the first step in building your following—congratulations! Next, we will look at the one thing that a leader's relationships will affect most significantly—culture. Leadership creates culture. So now, after building your relational muscle, you are ready to take the next step in pro leadership. Let's go!

─────────── **Principle Application** ───────────

1. What relationship(s) do you consider primary to your life?

2. How does that relationship make you a better leader?

3. What is the primary benefit you bring to that relationship?

4. Using the assessment questions found at the end of this chapter, how does this relationship line up in light of them?

6 | Leadership Creates Culture

*"Culture is what is left after everything we
have learned has been forgotten."*
—G. Bromley Oxnam

> **PRO LEADERSHIP PRINCIPLE:** First, leadership
> creates the culture.

Another one of my heroes is George Washington—one of the
first among our country's Founding Fathers. In that role, he
set a number of precedents that went on to strongly influence
the culture—and the trajectory—of the United States as a
nation. One of these was when he chose not to become king,
but rather to become president, and then to limit his tenure
to two terms. His leadership decision established an important precedent and set the course for the nation's future leaders. Like Washington, every entrepreneurial leader is setting
a course and establishing a culture. And that is what we are
going to talk about in this chapter: how leaders create culture
within their organizations, communities, and nations.

Your leadership, too, creates a specific culture. That is why,
on the journey to pro leadership, we must gain an awareness

and an understanding of who we are and of whom we were created to be. One of the first things you will create as a leader is the culture of your organization. In the end, that culture will be the validation (or the demise) of your leadership.

Perhaps you find yourself leading a start-up, as Washington did, or leading a turn-around, as Nelson Mandela did in South Africa. Or, you may be stepping into a new role with the objective of taking your team or your organization to the next level with a fresh vision. Whatever the case, culture should become your first priority. If you inherit a culture as a result of a leadership transition, your first decision will still be about culture: either you will keep it the way it is and grow it, or you will change it to something different. But whichever you choose, as a leader, culture is on you. From the moment you step into a leadership role, it is your responsibility.

On your journey to pro leadership, the culture you create will do more to determine your following than any other single thing you will do. As pro leader Peter Drucker wrote, "Culture eats strategy for breakfast." When I first read his words, I said, "No way can this be true!" Later, after I had spent a few semesters in the school of hard knocks as a new CEO, I said, "How did he know that?" Obviously, experience taught him, just as it did me.

Three Things to Remember about Corporate Culture

Much of my business experience has been building culture. I've learned a lot along the way. Sometimes I did the right thing and sometimes I did the wrong thing, but in each case,

I learned. As the saying goes, "We all make mistakes, but our mistakes don't need to make us." This is true! The reality that leadership creates culture (whether good, bad, or ugly!) is one of the most foundational lessons I learned.

Three principles combined to form this lesson:

1. Some cultures are functional, and some are dysfunctional, but leadership creates them both.
2. Culture trumps strategy.
3. You cannot change a culture without changing the people.

Effective leadership requires a working understanding of all three points. So, moving from general to specific, let's take a look at each:

First, positive cultures are functional, not dysfunctional. I don't know of one leader who did not set out to create a positive, functional culture. How else could you succeed in the long run? No one sets out to create a dysfunctional culture, and none I have been a part of started that way, but they became that way due to leadership decisions. Some were mine. Those decisions were almost entirely related to people, and how they were or were not handled.

The most common way for a culture to move toward dysfunction is valuing the business more than its people. Or, valuing one individual, which leads to the exclusion of the team or the business. This tension, between the value of the people and the value of the enterprise, is one of a leader's primary responsibilities.

Under the umbrella of a functional culture, three common threads run through it and all of them are related to people.

The first is growth—it is either promoted or inhibited. The second is freedom—it is either promoted or denied. The third is openness—healthy cultures are open and not closed off.

Functional cultures exist where growth is encouraged. In healthy and thriving corporate cultures, the soil of the organization is healthy and accepting of change. In these cases, leadership desires growth and is confident and secure enough to allow it. No organization will prosper for long unless its people are allowed and encouraged to grow in it.

Cultivating a Functional Culture

Growth happens in many ways, but a primary way is by giving your team authority equal to their responsibilities. This allows them to learn how to win by giving them the right to lose and, as a result, to learn from the experience.

Having and granting the freedom to fail is one of the greatest assets a leader can possess (and exercise). It is a critical asset in the development of other leaders. Fear of failure, on the other hand, causes paralysis that needs to be overcome in order to grow. Leaders must learn, and as Winston Churchill said, "Success is not final, failure is not fatal: it is the courage to continue that counts."

One of my favorite questions to ask people is, "What would you do if you knew you couldn't fail?" They generally respond first with a long pause, then a chuckle and a dismissive comment. I ask it again, truly wanting to uncover the real desire within the person. (I like to say this question is always an exercise in excavation before elevation!) After a period of silence (I'm not going to say another word until they do), the person will usually say, "Well, if I knew I couldn't fail, I would do . . ."

My follow-up is always, "So, why don't you do it?"

I have asked this question countless times and the answer is nearly always the same. Their answer is often motivated by a fear of failure, and typically, it is an irrational fear.

One entrepreneur I coached, who was facing a road block, answered my question by saying, "I would move my company to Colorado." When I asked him why he didn't, he said he was fearful that a move across country wouldn't work. We talked through many of the pluses and minuses, and he realized his fears were largely irrational. A week later he called me from Denver, where he had just signed a lease for a new headquarters space. They would begin the move a month later. Today, headquartered in Colorado, the business is thriving.

That is an example of a culture of freedom. The opposite is a culture of dependence. A dependent culture is a dysfunctional culture because it cannot prosper apart from its leader. Dependent cultures not only kill the ambition of the people and the organization, they will ultimately drain the energy of the leader and result in the burnout that has killed so many promising careers.

Every dependent culture I have seen or experienced has exhibited one glaring characteristic: responsibility without authority. Consider this: have you ever been given responsibility for an outcome but then discovered you did not have the authority to execute what needed to be done, to successfully carry out the mission you were responsible for? A simple example is the leader who raises the bar on sales expectations, but at the same time cuts the travel and marketing budgets. Today, whenever I am asked to accept responsibility, I always ask if I will have the authority to do what needs to be done. If the answer is no, I know that most likely the culture is a dependent one, but if the answer is yes, then the opposite is most likely true—it is a culture of freedom. The lesson learned is freedom creates its own success while dependence kills it. As a pro leader, the principle of responsibility with authority is a good barometer of the type of culture you are building.

Think about your leadership and about your team. When your leaders come to you, do they tell you what they have done, or do they ask you if they *may* do something? Do they have an owner mindset or an employee mindset? An owner has two things: responsibility and authority. An employee feels responsible for a task, but they may not feel they have authority to build beyond today. The owner mindset is a freedom mindset, while the employee mindset is one of dependence. The typical motivation behind an employee mindset is fear—that is, fear of failure or fear of being judged negatively for the work they are doing. I have found this mindset to be common among individuals who grew up in an environment where they felt valued only because of their results and not for who they were. Determining the mindset of your team members is a simple question that accurately diagnoses whether a culture is based on freedom or dependence.

The result of a freedom mindset will be a functional culture of openness—not just open in the sense of communication, but systemically open as opposed to closed. What I mean is this: in a closed system, nothing additional can be added to it. There is no room for growth, there is no room for expansion, there is no room for innovation. An open system, on the other hand, is growth oriented. There is room for new ideas, new processes and procedures, and continuous improvement. New ideas are embraced and given full consideration. The egos of those who have built what *is* do not stand in the way of what *might be*. The result of this type of environment is a nurturing culture that produces and develops good leaders.

Culture Trumps Strategy

No matter how well orchestrated your strategy, if the culture you have created doesn't support it, long-term success is not possible. Things might look good for a moment, but it won't last.

Experience taught me this lesson. When we merged our company, I believed we could combine our entrepreneurial culture with the big-company culture of our partner and have the best of both worlds. I was wrong. What happened was that our entrepreneurial culture was suffocated by the big company culture, and at the same time our partner's big company culture was de-railed by our entrepreneurial culture. We ended up with the worst of both worlds. As a result, the strategy that led to the merger failed. The responsibility was on me—lesson learned. The culture trumped strategy.

In the thirty-plus years I spent working in and leading investment management organizations, I was exposed to some of the greatest companies and their leaders. Because we grew to be a significant investor in many of those companies, few management teams came through our backyard without offering to meet with us. We always met with those we invested in and with those we would consider investing in. Over time, I made some observations about these organizations and the people who led them. I distilled my observations into three categories of companies:

1. those that have strong leaders but poor products
2. those that have weak leaders but strong products
3. those that have strong leaders and strong products.

In my experience, the investment opportunity was different with each, and over any period of time, a single company could fall into each of the categories. Strong company leadership today did not mean that would be true tomorrow, and the same was true about products. That is why, as investors, we focused as much attention on a company's leaders as we did on its product or service—because, as we learned, leadership creates culture, and culture trumps strategy.

Apple is an excellent example of a company that has occupied each category as a direct result of its leaders and the culture they created. In the beginning, Apple had strong leadership, but poor products—not bad products, just poor, due to the narrow focus of their market. As the company developed and suffered growing pains, the strong leader, Steve Jobs, was replaced. At the time, Apple's products were gaining traction, but a strong leader had been replaced by a weak one. Then Jobs returned, and with him, the Apple culture. Apple is one of the most valuable companies in the world. Why? Because out of the creative, customer-centered culture Apple's leadership created have come products and a company that have literally changed the world.

It's important to point out that culture won't change unless the people do. This is a principle all pro leaders must embrace if they are to build a lasting and positive culture. Now, I want to be clear what I am *not* saying. I don't mean you need to replace people; I mean they must change if the culture is going to change. Does that mean some no longer fit? Yes, that will always be the case, and where that is the case, that individual would not be successful in the new culture. (When that happens, please move them on in a just and fair way, to open another door of opportunity for them.)

But that being said, I believe almost all people are capable of change if they are given a clear vision to follow and they buy into it. When they understand the personal benefit(s) they will experience as a result of the change, the desire to do so will come from within. At that point, you have won their hearts and their minds. This transformation is what makes change possible. So, transforming a culture begins with the transformation of the people who make it up. Some transformations will be small, while others will be large, some will be fast, and others will take more time.

Transforming people requires transforming their minds— changing the way they think. This requires that, as a leader, you understand the three questions all people ask before following a leader: 1) Do you like me? 2) Can you help me? 3) Can I trust you? Once these three questions are affirmed, the individuals on your team will be open to the cultural transformation necessary to win.

But before individual transformations can begin, it is necessary to assess a company's culture and the people that represent it. Three questions you need to answer before deciding what steps to take toward building your culture are:

- Do my people fit my culture?
- Does my culture fit my people?
- Do I have people with a problem, or do I have problem people?

These questions are easier to answer in the start-up stage when you are dealing with fewer people and, as the leader, you are naturally closer to the day-to-day operation of the business. But as the business grows and people may join your team due to a skill they possess, they may not necessarily be a good cultural fit. I have found the first two questions to be helpful in the hiring process and the last two helpful in assessing associates who are already integrated into your culture. Let's look at these three questions separately:

Do my people fit my culture? Adding a new person into an established culture is similar to adding a new roommate. You need to think about how the new person will fit in. Will they add positively to the existing culture? On the other hand, if, as a leader, you determine the culture needs a change, then how well would your current team fit into the culture you envision? These are simple questions that are often difficult to answer. Nonetheless, it is important to the overall health of your culture to answer them.

Does my culture fit my people? Have you ever gone clothes shopping, tried something on, and although it fit well, you just didn't fit *it*? It wasn't your style. That's what I mean by this question. Let me give you a personal example. As I mentioned earlier, over a five-year period I commuted weekly to New York, where the merged headquarters of my firm were based. It was a valuable experience. I appreciate New York, but I am not a New Yorker. The culture did not fit me. I am 100 percent Midwest. It is not enough to know, *Does this person fit our culture?* You also need to know if your culture will fit the person. If you can answer yes to both questions your probability of success will increase greatly.

Do I have people with a problem, or do I have problem people? As a leader, you will eventually face this question.

Although I believe the answer is simple, it is not easy. I have tried and failed many times to fix problem people. I have learned that the best solution for problem people is to move them on. Give them what help you can, but don't allow them to remain and pollute your culture. On the other hand, people with a problem can normally be helped by helping them to solve their problem.

These three cultural questions fall into one of the most common leadership categories: problems to solve or tensions to manage. As a leader, more often than not, problems will be solved by your team members and what comes across your desk will be the tensions that need to be managed. They are the gray areas, and those are the decisions that define leadership. But in the end, it is those decisions—and your leadership—that create your culture.

Creating culture doesn't happen overnight. It is a daily discipline of consistently living the culture you desire to build. As a leader you will need patience, perspective, and proper expectations: patience with yourself and your team, and the perspective of time and proper expectations about the magnitude of your culture building. In the end, culture building will build your following.

But, like so much of life, building culture is a people business. That's why the next step a pro leader takes in building her following is leading from EQ, not IQ. That is what the next chapter is all about.

——————————— **Principle Application** ———————————

1. Briefly describe the culture your leadership has created.

2. If you were starting from scratch is this the culture you would aspire to? Why or why not?

3. What do you believe would help to build a stronger culture in your organization?

4. Are you willing to do what it takes? If so, what will be your first step(s)?

7 | Allow Your EQ to Lead

"EQ is the new IQ."
—Phil Styrlund

> **PRO LEADERSHIP PRINCIPLE:** IQ builds products but EQ builds following.

Success in the institutional investment world requires, among other things, a team with big-league horsepower, and that means brain power. The firm I started with had it—big time. The problem with high IQ, however, is it does not always come with high EQ—that is, emotional and relational intelligence, i.e., people skills.

Case in point: at one company I worked for, one of our lead portfolio managers (PM) was brilliant. His investment results matched those of Warren Buffett, but, like so many geniuses I have met, he was not comfortable with people. He also had a strange knack for saying the wrong thing, especially at the wrong time! A firm company rule required he never be allowed to visit a client or a prospect alone.

One day, one of the firm's most important clients, a prominent public fund, requested a meeting with this PM. It was a special meeting for new investment committee members and, being the top performer of their managers, they wanted to meet him. It should have been nothing but a gathering of the mutual admiration society, but it wasn't. Why? On the particular date the meeting was scheduled, all senior client relationship professionals—who would have normally traveled with this PM—were committed to other meetings. The CEO reasoned that since this was an unscheduled meet and greet only, and since investment results were so strong, the risk of sending this PM alone was small. Bad decision.

The day after the meeting, I was called into my boss's office. Seated in the corner with his head down and his hands folded was the PM. The two men had just finished a conference call with the chairman of our client's investment committee. The meeting with the PM had not gone well, and the new committee members were upset and questioning the wisdom of retaining our services. My boss handed me a plane ticket and said, "I want you to fix this. You are leaving in two hours and you are having dinner with the chairman and the new committee members."

I promptly flew out, had dinner, flew back, and the next morning was again called to my boss's office. He was alone and had just hung up from a call with our client. All was well. I don't remember what I did or said at the dinner, but I do remember it being a good relational time. Some serious talks, but also a couple of good laughs—I had fun and it was obvious they did too.

Before I left his office, I asked my boss, "Why did you send me?" After all, I was not a senior person at the firm, rather the CEO's personal assistant. He looked me straight in the eye and said, "Because people like you. Now, get back to work."

It wasn't until years later, leading my own firm, that I understood I had a well developed skill, and it was EQ. It was an executive coach, Bill Berman, who helped me to understand that good leaders have to develop this quality and let it lead.

"As you build this company," Bill said, "You must allow your EQ to lead the band."

Phil Styrlund of Summit Strategies, a business school for sales people, consults with only ten multinational clients at a time. He is the go-to expert on developing a global sales organization. It was Phil who said, "EQ is the new IQ." This is absolutely true. If you are a leader who desires to go pro, you must build a following and to do so, relational skills, emotional intelligence, people skills, and all the related soft skills adding up to EQ. And here is another truth: you cannot hire this out. You have got to have it yourself, and, if you don't, you will need to develop it.

The good news is, everyone can develop their EQ. Unlike IQ, which is pretty much what it is, EQ can be grown and developed. In the remainder of this chapter we are going to take time to assess your EQ and then look at EQ in three ways: why it matters to leadership, leading different EQ/IQ types, and developing your leadership EQ, both in your organization and in yourself.

Assessing Your EQ

The best place to start any endeavor is right where you are today. How would you assess your EQ? Are you emotionally intelligent? How are your relational skills? In Chapter Two, you spent time getting to know yourself, and in Chapter Five, you considered your relationships. Start by looking back at those self-assessments. This will help you to get your arms around your own EQ. You may also take on online EQ test—I have taken three and they all gave similar results.

I believe these tests are directionally correct, but like so many online tests, it is better to treat them like perfume: smell but don't swallow. After all, the truth is most often found a little deeper inside yourself. In my coaching practice, I prefer to focus on the results of the three assessments I mentioned in Chapter 3. This helps in your development by allowing you to tailor a development process suited to you alone. Leadership development is best when it is tailor made and not off the rack.

No matter what your score (and on which test), as a leader you owe it to yourself and your followers to develop and strengthen your EQ. In my experience, no development has had a greater impact on my leadership and on the leadership of my clients than this.

Why EQ Matters to Leadership

In his book, *The 21 Irrefutable Laws of Leadership*, John Maxwell, in explaining the Law of Influence, writes, "The true measure of leadership is influence—nothing more, nothing less." The truth of this statement has been proven time and again by my own experience. Pro leaders must have the ability to influence others to follow them, and the most important ingredient in influence is relationship. The key to a winning relationship is winning the heart, and doing so is not possible without EQ. You may have a high IQ, and natural giftedness in your vocation, but if you are unable to influence others, you may be effective as a manager, but you will never be a leader.

Remember, leadership is about people, and people will follow with their head for only so long before they eventually grow weary and peel off or fade away. But if, through your relational abilities, they feel your love and care for them, they will follow you even when times get tough. That is why it is vital to your leadership to allow your EQ to lead.

But EQ alone won't be enough. In fact, it must be balanced with IQ. Although IQ is not a natural leader attribute, and as a result is best relegated to the back seat, it is important to the success of any enterprise. Your role as leader will be to balance both EQ and IQ, to manage the balance and tension between the two. That balance/tension will be manifested through how your team works together. Recall that EQ builds companies and IQ builds products; it is not possible to have one without the other. At the same time, one is not valued over and above the other. Although the theme of this lesson is to let your EQ lead, that does not make it more valuable than IQ—both are required to win.

EQ + IQ = 3 Types of Players

When filtering for EQ and IQ, there are three categories of people you will find. I have worked with, followed, or led all of these: EQ dominant, IQ dominant, and EQ/IQ flexible. A strong culture, a strong organization, and a strong team will have all three types of players on their roster. Where the two dominant types will normally be position players, most pro leaders will be flexible. Let me explain.

To be great a company, you must add value through offering a great product. IQ builds products. People who are IQ dominant have high IQs—a natural gift which, when applied, results in great products that add value to people's lives. Consider the advances in medicine, science, and technology. None would have been possible without the work of IQ-dominant people.

In my own experience in the investment management industry, investment results were our product, and those results were driven almost entirely by portfolio managers and analysts, the vast majority of whom were IQ-dominant individuals. Often, the best among them were successful largely due to the fact that they rarely allowed emotion to affect their investment decisions. From a leadership standpoint, I looked at these IQ-dominant individuals as position players; they made up our equivalent of an engineering department. They were our design engineers. As a group, these people had no interest in leadership, but would quickly follow a strong leader and just as quickly abandon a weak one.

To successfully lead an IQ-dominant player, you will need to first satisfy their intellect, through a clear and rational articulation of your vision and your strategy. Next, they need to be enlisted in forming the tactics you will employ to accomplish the strategy. Since they are the product designers, they will want to have shared ownership of the product before they will follow your lead and buy into your vision. Once you have satisfied their intellect, you are free to win their hearts.

The second player type is the EQ-dominant individual. This person is also a position player. You will most often find them in advertising and creative positions, client service, marketing, and sales—critical roles if a company is to be successful. Rarely will they build a product, but their EQ is invaluable in product development, specifically in refining products in order to bring forward the product the market is demanding. These individuals are valuable because they understand the basic truth that no one has ever bought anything; they are sold on something. As Pat Fallon and Fred Senn, co-founders of Fallon, one of the worlds most renowned creative agencies, wrote in their book by the same name, these people know how to *Juice the Orange.*

To lead EQ-dominant players, a leader must always start with the heart. You must offer a creative vision and strategy, and they must see you as the courage behind the plan. They want to be led, from their heart to their head. And while you must appeal first to their creative side, you may not ignore their rational side, because that is where their fears exist. As their leader, they will naturally look to you for courage and to help them overcome their fears.

The third type of player on your roster will be what I define as EQ/IQ flexible. Every great leader I have met or studied fell into this category. The defining characteristic of this person is her ability to balance EQ and IQ—specifically, having the ability to discern which attribute needs application to a particular circumstance and to execute the proper timing of the use of the attribute. In athletics, this is called hand-eye coordination. All athletes have it in one degree or another, and the degree to which they have it is what separates the amateur from the professional. EQ/IQ flexible personalities have the ability to walk into a room and judge immediately the chemistry of the room and then, to activate the attribute most suited to the current environment. Whether a board room or a lunch room, they are comfortable in both environments, because they have the ability to adapt instantly to each environment.

This is my personality type and, as a result, I find these people the most difficult to lead. Nevertheless, to lead EQ/IQ personalities effectively, start with their heart by appealing to their deepest motivations. But don't stop there. You will need to follow with the logical argument as you clearly build your case. If you win them to your cause, they will become your greatest ally, because they will naturally become spokespersons for that cause. However, this is a two-edged sword. If you lose their trust—or if they simply do not accept your vision and the mission—it may hinder their work. In the end, these personalities are a strong proof-source of the truth that the true measure of leadership is influence—nothing more, nothing less.

Developing EQ in Yourself and Others

Okay, we have answered why leadership EQ matters, and we have defined the three types of EQ/IQ players you will lead and how to lead them. It is time now to look at how EQ is developed in your culture, on your team, and in yourself.

Developing a culture of EQ starts where every other cultural development starts, with leadership. That would be *you*. Based on the principle you read about in the last chapter—Leadership Creates Culture—to develop a culture-wide EQ you will need to start with yourself, beginning with your attitude toward the people you are leading. As humans, we naturally favor ourselves. That means, if I am an EQ-dominant person, I will naturally be drawn to other EQ-dominant people. The same is true for the IQ-dominant person. This is fine for friendships. However, favoring one trait over the other in your organization will create a culture of favoritism, resulting in dysfunction caused by this imbalance. As the leader, it is critical for you to have no favorites, being able to defend both camps. You must not have any favorites.

When I coach leaders or consult organizations who desire to develop a leadership culture, I like to start where I did with my company, with *Strengths Finder*. When I took the Strengths Finder assessment and first learned my "strengths," I was intrigued, and immediately ordered a copy of the book for each of my senior leaders. They each took the assessment, then we plotted our strengths on a chart. The next step was doing the exercise again, only this time with the entire firm. Then we used, *Strengths-Based Leadership*, Tom Rath and Barry Conchie's follow-up book to *Strengths Finder 2.0*. The cultural effect this decision had was significant. It was relational gold, EQ over IQ. The results, which we shared with all, were built into a spreadsheet and plotted on a graph (which appealed to our IQ dominant associates), but the emotional effect was even greater. It was an example of caring, inclusive leadership.

As a leader desiring to develop cultural EQ, there are other assessments that may have a similar effect, but I like this one for three important reasons:

1. It is simple to understand and easy to execute.
2. It is available to anyone at any time.
3. It is fast and fun.

I have recommended this exercise to many leaders and, in following-up with those who executed it, the feedback is almost entirely positive.

Developing EQ among your leadership team is a necessary activity of pro leadership. Pro leaders realize they cannot succeed alone. As John Maxwell astutely commented, "If you want to go fast, go alone; if you want to go far, go with others." The extent to which you foster EQ among the members of your inner circle is the extent to how far your leadership team will go. To do this as a leader, you will need to start at the same place you did with your cultural EQ: your attitude. Leadership development of any type is a process, not a destination, a journey that never ends. When you stop developing, you stop growing.

In the wonderful book, *Think and Grow Rich*, written by Napoleon Hill and underwritten by Andrew Carnegie (who desired to encourage so many who had lost everything as a result of the Great Depression), the idea of the Mastermind Group is introduced as a catalyst of personal growth. I recommend to my clients that they form a Mastermind Group with their senior leaders and use it as a personal and leadership development tool. You can always work individually with your leaders to help them grow, and you should, but when a small group of leaders grow together, great things can be accomplished.

I encourage you to take the first step. Gather your senior leadership team and share with them your desire to form a Mastermind Group for the purpose of growing together in leadership. It should be a small group, seven is perfect, as long as they are all there. Start with a twelve-week course, ninety minutes, once a week for twelve weeks. Pick your favorite book on leadership and take a chapter a week and lead the discussion. Answer these four questions:

1. What does it say?
2. What does it mean?
3. What does it mean to me?
4. What does it mean to this organization?

It is okay for you to be the leader as long as you remember to keep your mouth shut and your ears open, and as long as you give your team the freedom to speak openly. This means that anything they say will not be used against them once the session is over.

There are times and teams where it is best to have an outsider lead your Mastermind. If you have a coach, ask her or him if he/she would lead it for you. Whatever the required investment, it will be worth it. If you are not leading, some believe it's best if you are not there, but that depends on your individual circumstance and your relationship with your team. Ask your coach what he/she thinks.

Last but not least, no matter what your own EQ level, ongoing personal development is always important. Read all you are able to find on the topic. Second, if you don't have one, get a coach. (As I wrote the above words, I was remembering it was my coach who taught me how vital it was that I develop my EQ, and that I allow it to lead.) Third, join a peer group or start one yourself. It is true that iron sharpens iron. Developing EQ is not a solo sport, you will need to have some people to rub up against. Leadership is a lonely business; you need to have someone to talk to, a safe environment to share, and you also need people who will tell you the last 10 percent, that which most people won't tell you. A coach, a therapist, or a Mastermind Group may provide that for you.

In summary, IQ builds products, but EQ builds companies and followings. So, as you step out today to lead, let your EQ lead the way. Develop your EQ, your culture's, your team's, and your own. Do so, and you will have taken a big step in developing your following and your pro leadership abilities, putting yourself in a prime position to be able to motivate the people you lead.

─────────── **Principle Application** ───────────

1. How would you rate your EQ? Do you tend to be EQ dominant? IQ dominant? EQ/IQ flexible?

2. How has your EQ influenced (or perhaps hindered) your
   leadership?

3. After reading this chapter, have you gleaned any ways you
   could strengthen your EQ in order to make you a more
   effective leader?

4. Take a moment to do a quick mental assessment of the
   team you lead. Which team members are EQ dominant?
   Which are IQ dominant? Which are flexible?

5. Note any ways you might lead/communicate with these
   individuals differently.

8 | Be a Motivator

"Such is man, and so must he be understood by those who would lead him, even to his own best interests."
—Abraham Lincoln

> **PRO LEADERSHIP PRINCIPLE:** Positive, tailor-made motivation builds following.

One month before he died, I received a letter from my father and, along with it, a copy of a speech by Abraham Lincoln. It had hung on the wall in his bedroom, next to the chair he sat in each morning to put on his shoes. Over the years, I often watched as he would pause and read it before he left for work. As a result, he had memorized it.

In his letter to me, my dad shared the positive effect of Lincoln's principles on his leadership of his sales team—some six hundred people—and said he hoped these principles would help me too in my own leadership career. He encouraged me to memorize the speech, because that was the best way to ensure it would come out in my leadership.

I have carried that speech with me for over thirty years, although I confess I cannot recite it word perfectly like Dad could. However, I have internalized its leadership principles and have witnessed them playing out in my life as I lead others. As I have studied leadership, influence, and motivation, nothing I have read or heard is better than the two hundred thirty-one words Abraham Lincoln spoke over one hundred and seventy-five years ago:

> *When the conduct of men is designed to be influenced, persuasion—kind, unassuming persuasion—should ever be adopted. It is an old and a true maxim "that a drop of honey catches more flies than a gallon of gall." So with men. If you would win a man to your cause, first convince him that you are his sincere friend. Therein is a drop of honey that catches his heart, which, say what you will, is the great high road to his reason, and which, when once gained, you will find but little trouble in convincing his judgment of the justice of your cause, if indeed that cause really be a just one. On the contrary, assume to dictate to his judgment, or to command his action, or to mark him as one to be shunned and despised, and he will retreat within himself, close all the avenues to his head and his heart; and though your cause be naked truth itself, transformed to the heaviest lance, harder than steel and sharper than steel can be made, and though you throw it with more than herculean force and precision, you shall be no more able to pierce him than to penetrate the hard shell of a tortoise with a rye straw. Such is man, and so must he be understood by those who would lead him, even to his own best interests.*

Lincoln's wisdom is remarkable and timeless, and his ability to communicate unsurpassed. He knew what was required to motivate people. The basic principles are all here.

As C.S. Lewis once said, "If we fail to keep the first things first, we will lose not only the first things, but the second things as well." Nowhere is this truer than in leadership and the art of motivation.

Lincoln's Seven Principles of Leadership

Seven leadership principles stand out in Lincoln's speech. Let's take a look at each:

- the principle of conduct
- the principle of design
- the principle of influence
- the principle of persuasion
- the principle of friendship
- the principle of justice
- the principle of respect

1. *"When the **conduct** of men . . ."*

   First is the principle of **conduct**, or the behavior of people. Our conduct is the result of many influences, but all fall under one of two broad categories: nature or nurture. Nature says our conduct, or our behavior, is a result of the world we have been born into. You cannot help the time, the place, and the circumstances of your birth, or the environment into which you were placed. Nurture is the family or the tribe into which you were born and the way they impact your choices. You did not get to choose it, but that environment is a big reason why you behave the way you do.

In order to motivate others, we must understand this basic principle and its effect on an individual's behavior. It is important to understand the people we lead, and to recognize that they often don't see things the way we see them; they see things through the lens of their own perceptions, values, and worldview. How a person thinks and behaves, and who a person is in his or her inner being, is the direct result of where they have come from, whether it is due to their "nature" or "nurture." Pro leaders recognize this and make an effort to truly know their followers.

2. *... is designed ...*

The second ingredient of motivation is **design**. Motivation is not a random act; rather, it should be planned with a specific goal in mind. People will not follow a leader who doesn't know the way. Leadership is a journey that must be planned, and that plan is first *designed* by the leader. Lincoln is saying that motivation must be strategic. Know your audience, know yourself, and know your plan.

3. *... to be influenced ...*

The third ingredient in motivation is the principle of **influence**. As John Maxwell has said, "Leadership is influence." That is the end you desire when you motivate: to influence conduct. The politician desires to influence the conduct of the voter, the coach desires to influence the conduct of his players, and the leader desires to influence the conduct of her followers.

When you are in a position to motivate others, you are accepting the great privilege and great responsibility that comes with being an influencer.

4. *. . . **persuasion**, kind, unassuming persuasion, should ever be adopted.*
The principle of persuasion is the fourth ingredient of effective motivation. Persuasive motivation is distinct from forceful motivation (which is otherwise known as authoritarianism, or even downright dictatorship). Persuasion, on the other hand—and as Lincoln pointed out—is kind, gentle, and unassuming. Authoritarianism may be muscled or forced, but persuasion is natural and unforced. It is influence with patience.

5. *. . . first convince him that you are **his sincere friend**.*
Friendship is the next of Lincoln's principles. This concept is born out of another leadership principle: no one cares how much you know until they know how much you care. It is an inborn human desire and longing to be loved and accepted. To effectively influence and motivate someone, they must feel you care for them. Friends listen to friends; they hear them and as a result will more easily follow a sincere friend's leadership. Leadership begins and ends with people. Friendship is the drop of honey that wins the heart.

6. *. . . of the **justice** of your cause, if indeed that cause really be a just one.*
Justice is the sixth ingredient necessary for motivation to be effective. Human beings have an innate sense of justice and require it before they will follow a

leader. A cause must be proven just from the start. If you cannot prove your cause to be a reasonable one, you will not be trusted, and you will not be able to motivate your followers in the long term, no matter what you do.

There was a parenting philosophy in generations past that went generally along the lines of "Because I said so." As psychologists have discovered in recent years, this philosophy did a great deal more harm than good for the children to which it was applied. Not only does it not work in parenting; it doesn't work in any other setting! While people may not need to know all the reasons why you do (or ask) the things you do, they do deserve to be made reasonably aware of the general "why" behind your actions and requests.

7. . . . *or to command his action, or to mark him as one to be shunned and despised* . . .
The final principle found in Lincoln's speech is the principle of **respect**. I had a boss and mentor who taught me a leadership lesson on this topic I will never forget. "Andy," he said, "this is not the army, these people don't have to come to work each day." Understanding this truth helped me answer the question, *What motivates these people to come here each day?* In the beginning, I thought it was money, but I soon learned that while money often attracted people initially, it was rarely enough to keep them. To keep them, I had to give them more, and "more" began with respecting them.

Respect who your people are, respect where they have been, respect their efforts, and respect their opinions. I have learned that when I respect others, they will more readily respect me, and that makes leadership a lot easier.

Applying Lincoln's Seven Principles

Now that we have established some solid principles of motivation, we are ready to move on to their application. "Process follows principles" is another good maxim for pro leadership. Your leadership will rise or fall based upon the principles on which it is founded. Your processes will also succeed or fail based upon those same principles. Remember that processes evolve, but principles remain the same.

I've found that applying Lincoln's principles of motivation is a four-step leadership process, aiming to motivate your individual followers one at a time. That's right, one at a time. Leaders don't motivate companies or organizations; they motivate people, and, to be effective, you must consider your individual followers. The four steps are simple: 1) start with yourself, 2) move from your inner circle out, 3) always begin with your "possibility thinkers," and 4) always be motivating.

Like everything in leadership, the most important person you must motivate effectively is yourself, so that is where all motivational leadership starts. Let's apply the seven principles personally, so you may learn to motivate *yourself* first:

1. **Conduct** is what you expect from yourself, or what you know needs to happen for you to get to where you are going. To start with yourself, you have to know yourself. The earlier exercises you went through to answer the question, *Who am I?* will help you here. If you know

who you are, and you know your why, you know what motivates you. Feed yourself with what motivates you.

2. **Design** is an anticipation of your need to be motivated, and being strategic about it. Make a plan for each day and allow the time and space in your life for the disciplines you need to be effective at what you do. Whatever those disciplines include for you (e.g., reading, study, exercise, prayer or meditation, quality time with primary relationships, etc.), remember that motivation is not an accident; it must be planned.

3. **Influence** yourself for your own good. I will often hear a coaching client say, "I should do this or that." I have learned to say, "Stop 'should-ing' all over yourself!" What do you *want* to do; what would be the best choice right now? What choice gives you a sense of personal peace and satisfaction? Let that choice influence you. Remember the acronym WIN: **W**hat's **I**mportant **N**ow.

4. **Persuasion** is the inner voice urging you to be true to who you really are, to do what you were designed to do—bringing your true self to your leadership. Don't operate from a list of "shoulds," either self-imposed or from someone else. Operate from your "why."

5. **Friendship,** on a personal level, is liking who you are and being okay with what you learned when you answered the question, *who am I?* After all, it's hard to have great friendships with others if you don't have one with yourself.

6. **Justice** is revealed by the passion you feel as you consider your leadership. Motivation comes easily to those who feel their cause is a just one. When I want to consider the justice of a cause I have a simple rule: if my

cause benefits others, it is most likely a just one, on the other hand, if it benefits only me, it is doubtful it could be called just. Justice is not selfish.

7. **Respect** yourself. You can hardly respect others if you do not respect yourself. I am not talking about being narcissistic, self-absorbed, or selfish. Rather, respecting yourself simply means understanding your own human value and, as a result, treating yourself as well as you would treat others. One of the common issues of good leaders is they will often put others first to the detriment of themselves. Do this long enough and you can forget that you need to "put your own oxygen mask on first." I have seen too many leaders think so much of others that they forget about themselves, ultimately leading to negative consequences in all areas of their lives (including burnout, troubled relationships, stress, anxiety, and beyond). Remember, balance is necessary in all things.

Bringing It Home

These seven principles from Abraham Lincoln will help form a strong foundation for your ability to motivate others. As you build on your pro leadership abilities, I hope you will consider committing these principles to memory. Doing so would be a great building block in your own leadership transformation.

Consider how you may use these principles to motivate *yourself* first. Then, you will be ready to motivate your followers. Doing it with others is the logical next step; simply apply the seven principles in a process by asking questions you form around each of the principles, just like you did for yourself.

Start with your inner circle first. These are the members of your team you work most closely and most often with. They may be your senior leadership team. They may be your direct reports. Whatever your context, always begin on the inside and move out.

The reason for this is that motivation moves out—not in—and motivation creates momentum. Naturally, positive persuasion from you to your inner circle will then be transmitted to that leader's sphere of influence, and so on, like the ripples that move outward when a rock is thrown into the water. Motivation spreads! That is why it is critical that it be positive.

Start with your positive thinkers. I like to think of these people as the possibility thinkers. You know how it is—different personalities see things differently. Some personalities are glass half full and some are glass half empty. It is difficult to gain motivational momentum when you are working alone, and this is what happens when you seek to persuade a glass-half-empty person—or what I have shortened to a "no" personality. On the other hand, if you first motivate your possibility thinkers, or your "yes" personalities, they will aid you in winning over the "no" personalities over time.

Remember, as long as you are leading you will need to be motivating. It never ends! Influence is a form of motivation, so it would be correct to say leadership is motivation. For pro leaders, motivation is a part of them; they are always naturally motivating.

I encourage you to think about these seven principles together with your own leadership in mind. Answer these questions:

- What conduct do I desire to see from my followers?
- Understanding the individual backgrounds of each, what is each person's best form of motivation?
- What is the most positive way to influence my team toward our mutual goal?
- As a leader, do I most often persuade, or do I dictate?
- Would my followers say I care for them?
- Is my cause a just one, and can I communicate that it is?
- Do I demonstrate respect for each of my followers?

Answering these questions will help you to assess your motivational skill level and equip you to be more successful in the motivation of the people whom you desire to lead. Remember: building your following never ends!

And, now that you have gained some more tools to help you be a motivator, and have learned how to apply the pro leadership principle that positive tailor-made motivation will build your following, the next step is to lead your followers by applying your own experience to inspire and equip them. That is the subject of the next chapter: "Teach What You Know."

--------- **Principle Application** ---------

1. What type of motivation best moves you, personally?

2. What types of motivation do you resist?

3. What types of motivation have you utilized effectively in your leadership?

4. What type of motivation has been ineffective?

5. Using the diagnostic questions at the end of this chapter, assess your motivation quotient with the team of people you are currently leading.

9 | Teach What You Know (Teach Reality, Not Theory)

"To teach is to learn twice."
—Joseph Joubert

> **PRO LEADERSHIP PRINCIPLE:** You cannot teach what you do not know; you cannot lead if you have not learned.

When I was a young leader, I once uncovered a prospective client out of state who was conducting a search to find a manager for their pension fund. Our CEO had told me when he hired me, "You are a bird dog; you find them, and we will shoot them." Well, this was a big bird, and I didn't want to miss it.

The custom at our firm for these kinds of presentations was to bring along a portfolio manager to handle the investment portion of the presentation. As the business development person, I would "set the table" and then turn the presentation over to that portfolio manager, who would cover our investment process. Typically, it would be decided in advance which portfolio manager would be assigned this new client; then he or she would participate in the presentation. The size of the portfolio determined which portfolio manager would be assigned.

This prospective client portfolio, although large to me, was smaller than our firm average, and, as a result, warranted a more junior manager. However, on the date of the scheduled presentation, all were unavailable. The only person available that day was our founder, chief investment officer, and president. Dick Tschudy had founded the firm forty-seven years earlier and was considered an icon in the investment community. Until that day, I had rarely spent more than an hour alone with him. What was Dick like? Imagine *Star Wars*. Now, think of Obi-Wan Kenobi, the Jedi Master. That was Dick. Okay, now you have the picture.

The presentation was a ninety-minute drive from our office. We took Dick's Cadillac, and he asked me to drive. On the way there, he talked on the phone the whole time. When I interrupted him to ask if he would like to review the presentation book, he kindly replied, "No, thank you."

We arrived and he ended his call.

"Dick, how would you like to divide this presentation?" I asked.

"Andy, you introduce me, and I will handle the rest." That's what I did, and he did handle the rest. It was a presentation I will never forget.

When we were escorted to the anteroom outside the boardroom where the presentation was to take place, we passed one of our competitors, who had just finished their own presentation. They smiled at me, but their smiles quickly vanished when Dick came around the corner, and they nodded reverently and walked away. A few minutes later, Dick and I entered the boardroom and I walked around the table, giving a book to each of the seven committee members. When I handed a book to Dick, he set it down and folded his hands on top of it.

I introduced Dick and then sat back and watched a master at work. He talked about the founding of the firm, what had caused him to do it, and what he had learned in the last 47 years. Then, he talked about the four "Ps" of investment success: people, philosophy, process, and performance. He not only spoke to the how, but also to the why. He never did open the book, and he never looked away from the committee members, always keeping eye contact and a soft, confident smile with one of the members. Sixty minutes after we walked in, we walked out, and got back into the car for our ninety-minute drive home. This time, Dick drove.

"Do you have any questions about the presentation?" Dick asked me.

"Just one," I replied. "Why didn't you open the book?"

"I don't need the book," he replied. "I wrote it."

Five minutes into our drive, my cell phone rang. It was the CFO of the company calling to tell me they would like us to manage their portfolio. That call made the drive fun. Dick said, "Congratulations, you won a big one; good for you!" We both knew Dick had won, but he was a humble leader who always gave credit to others before taking any for himself.

Sadly, that was the last bit of time I would spend with him. A few days after our presentation, he was diagnosed with an acute strain of cancer, and three weeks later he passed away. Maybe it was his untimely death, or the fact that I was the last person at the firm to spend time with him in his "natural" environment, or the presentation itself, or maybe just his leadership, but I don't think I will ever forget him or that presentation.

The truth is: I knew that presentation cold, and as a result, could have given it in a technically perfect way, even hitting on some points that Dick had left out. But I don't believe my presentation would have been followed fifteen minutes later by a call from the prospect's CFO. Why? Because I had knowledge and Dick had experience, and the later has greater value than the former.

You Don't Know What You Don't Know

You cannot teach what you do not know; you cannot lead if you have not learned. You can know *about* something without actually really *knowing* it. Understanding the difference is a key to becoming a pro leader and crucial to building your following. Like so many lessons I have learned, this one came experientially, too.

I was a top producer at the firm where I started my career, and as happens to many in this situation, I was promoted into leadership—not due to my leadership abilities but because I was able to produce. When it happened, I was young, eager, and inexperienced, and I did not know that being a top producer did not necessarily make one a leader. After all, I had read many leadership books; how hard could it be? (Famous last words, right?)

You have read this story many times, no doubt: I failed miserably and did a lot of needless relational damage in the process. I was attempting to develop leaders using concepts I had never learned. I was put in a position of leadership, responsible for teaching something I did not know. My inexperience resulted in poor judgment and poor results. I was living proof that what Will Rogers said is true: "Good judgment comes from experience, and a lot of that comes from bad judgment."

It was the subsequent positive experience at that same firm, which I related at the opening of this chapter, that confirmed this principle and allowed me to learn it in such a way that it has been a part of my leadership ever since. I learned four lessons because of this experience:

1. Knowledge is not the same as experience.
2. People won't follow knowledge alone.
3. Wisdom = Who I am + My Why + Knowledge + Experience + Judgment
4. Do what you do best and hire the rest—80:20

First, I learned that knowledge is not the same as experience. Knowing about something is not the same as knowing something. When knowledge is applied, experience is the result and it is experience that gives one the ability to make judgments, and good judgment leads to wisdom. But without application, without experience, knowledge alone is impotent.

Secondly, I learned that people won't follow knowledge alone. They must have a strong sense of your ability to accomplish what you propose to lead them into. Your knowledge is assumed. If they don't believe you have it, they won't show up in the first place. Smart people desire to follow smart leaders. Leaders must have more than knowledge. Your experience will give your followers confidence that you are able to lead them to where they desire to go.

Thirdly, wisdom creates a following and is vital to maintaining a following. However, it doesn't come easily, nor can the process for gaining it be shortened. The formula I have learned is:

Wisdom = who am I + my why + knowledge + experience + judgment

The length of the formula is telling you wisdom takes time, and it is a step-by-step process that cannot be rushed.

In leadership, as in life, everything starts with knowing your-self and your why. From that foundation, you add knowledge, experience, and good judgment; wisdom is the outcome of this continuous process of personal growth.

The final and most practical lesson I learned regarding the principle of "teach what you know" is that it requires a com-mitment to the 80:20 principle. The 80:20 principle is true in a variety of contexts, but this is what it looks like in this one: no leader knows everything, so effective leaders focus on the 20 percent they know, and leave the 80 percent they only know *about* to others. In other words, do what you do best and hire the rest.

The Application to Your Leadership

When I coach leaders, the overall objective is to transform smart leaders into wise leaders. Wisdom is a necessary ingredi-ent of effective leadership. Today it is even more important than in the past, yet as always, it appears to be a rare commodity.

In today's economy, one that is defined by the "Ama-zonization" of everything—including the commodification of knowledge, the value of wisdom, or knowing what to do and when—far exceeds the value of knowing how to do some-thing. As Artificial Intelligence (AI) works its way into more areas of our lives and the economy, the hard skills of the past are going to AI and the old "soft skills"—wisdom, discern-ment, and emotional intelligence—have become the new hard skills. These are assets that will not be commoditized, and those who possess them will have a clear advantage over those who don't.

Am I saying we should ignore growing our base of knowledge? Of course not. To do so would be foolish. What Thomas Jefferson said over two hundred years ago is still true today: "When speaking about human growth" he said, "there are only three things that will make you any different two years from now then you are today: the books you read, the people you associate with, and the time you take to reflect on the first two."

Jefferson was a wise man; he was a reader, a relator, and a reflector. As he learned, he applied his new knowledge and he reflected on what he learned; doing so naturally grew wisdom in him. When Jefferson met someone, he always started with the same question, "What do you know more clearly today than the last time we met?" I borrow that question from Jefferson and use it at the start of every coaching session I conduct. It is a question meant to get to wisdom, which is a characteristic of someone who has the good judgment to apply knowledge when and where it can be most effective. When will it have its greatest impact? When will it have the greatest influence? This is key to building your following.

How It Works in Action

This principle "you cannot teach what you do not know" is closely related to another principle: people who know how follow those who know why. When these two principles come together, as they did in my example of Dick Tschudy, and as they do in so many other pro leaders, the combination gives power and credibility to their leadership. This naturally results in building a following. To understand why this happens, let's review the building blocks of pro leadership we have identified so far: self-knowledge, knowing your why, your knowledge base, your experience, your learned judgment, and your level of wisdom. This is what I call the wisdom pyramid.

Who you are is its foundation, and its first layer is your why. Once you have answered these two questions, you will naturally move to your highest and best calling. The next level is your base of knowledge; as you apply it, you gain experience and develop judgment. Together, these lead to wisdom, which is the highest and best attribute of a leader.

Now would be a good time to reflect and assess where you are on the leadership pyramid. A word of encouragement: I have learned that the final four steps—knowledge, experience, wisdom and judgment—are perennial and will remain so as long as you fertilize them with the books you read, the people you associate with, and your personal time of reflection and meditation.

Risks to Consider

I want to leave you with some words of warning and encouragement as you lead from your wisdom while you commit to teaching reality, not theory:

1. **Experience is not the best teacher, but sometimes it is the only teacher.**
   Sometimes learning on the job is the only option. This is a reality every entrepreneur and/or leader has faced. The important thing is to know you are learning as you go; you must come to know what you don't already know.

2. **Be careful of knowledge not backed by experience.**
   As I sit in my coaching chair, especially with new clients, I will often be asked, *Can you recommend a book so I can learn this?* Before I answer this, I invariably think of a friend of mine who read a book on day trading, and then proceeded to lose a significant portion of his nest egg applying the concepts in the book. Book knowledge is not everything and can even be detrimental when not combined with real-world experience.

3. **Don't go it alone—all of us are better than one of us.**
   No leader succeeds alone. If you have not already done so, build an inner circle of people whose knowledge, experience, judgment, and wisdom you may call on. As a coach, one of the major benefits I bring to my clients is the acknowledgment that I have failed so they won't have to.

The tough truth about asking these questions and considering these risks is that it may require a level of humility and vulnerability that makes you uncomfortable. I have been there too. Do it anyway; the benefit will be worth it.

But before you move on, I encourage you to answer two questions:

1. As I build my base of knowledge, how am I applying it to my leadership so that my experience will add wisdom?
2. As I develop the leaders around me, am I leading and teaching from a place of wisdom?

Always remember that reality—not theory—is a key attribute of wise leadership. It will benefit you greatly, because leading through wisdom results in peace and strength. You will communicate these qualities to your followers, they will benefit too, and will hopefully pass them along to others.

Bottom line: you will not be able to teach reality without being real yourself. That is the next building block in becoming a pro leader, and the subject of the next chapter.

——————— Principle Application ———————

1. Have you ever tried to teach something you had not experienced yourself? What was the result?

2. How has your experience made you a more effective leader?

3. How do you learn best?

4. What do you believe is the best teacher: a classroom or the real world? Why? How does this belief influence the methodology you use to teach other?

10 | Be Real (Lead with Integrity)

The supreme quality for leadership is unquestionably integrity. Without it, no real success is possible, no matter whether it is on a section gang, a football field, in an army, or in an office.
—Dwight D. Eisenhower

PRO LEADERSHIP PRINCIPLE: To be real is to lead with personal integrity.

The business I led was not quite ten years old, but we had experienced nice growth and as a result, had gained recognition as an up-and-comer in the wealth management industry. One of the investment research firms with which we did business was bringing WorldCom management to town to meet one-on-one with some large shareholders. We did not qualify for a one-on-one meeting, but we owned a two-percent position in all of our client portfolios. And, since we were a growing client, we were invited to a group meeting that would include a chance to ask questions of, and shake hands with, the CEO.

Normally, our chief investment officer would attend a meeting such as this, but he had a previous commitment, so I went in his place. I have always taken opportunities to meet leaders, and the CEO was a major business leader with a larger-than-life personality. He was a telecom billionaire, and

I was excited to meet him, hoping to learn something from being in the same room with him.

Since it was a last-minute invitation, I did not have time to do any homework on our ownership of the stock other than reading the notes on our rationale for the investment. The meeting was to start at 2:00 p.m. in a small meeting room at a downtown hotel. I arrived a few minutes early and was one of a couple dozen other small institutional investors who were also clients of the firm hosting the meeting. At 2:15, there was no CEO. At 2:30, still no CEO. At 2:35, he walked in, grabbed a Coke, made a few comments about the company, and then asked for questions. He took a few, but his answers were anything but straight. He also made it clear that they had a hard stop at 3:00 pm. With about ten minutes remaining, the questioning turned to his CFO, so the visiting CEO walked over to grab another Coke. So did I. With a Coke in one hand, I introduced myself to him. We chatted for not more than two minutes, but that two minutes resulted in our selling our entire position in the stock.

What happened? I don't consider myself a great stock picker, but I do know people. At the time, this CEO was one of the wealthiest men in America, a telecom titan. Yet, as he spoke to me, a young leader of a small but growing company, I couldn't help but notice that he could not look me in the eye, not once. In addition, he had a nervous response to my questions. He would not shoot straight with me or even answer the few simple questions my investment team had given me to ask him. He either did not know the answers, or he did not want to give them to me. *Why is he so nervous?* I wondered. I was struck with the thought that we should not be investing our clients' assets in someone like that, to do so would lack integrity on my own part!

As fate would have it, not long after that meeting, the wheels came off the company and the CEO was exposed as a fraud, convicted, and sent to federal prison for twenty-five years. Unfortunately, many investors lost much or all of their investment due to this man's lack of integrity. But thankfully, our clients did better than most, not because we were smarter, but because we put a premium on integrity and refused to invest where we did not see it demonstrated.

This experience was proof of the principle highlighted in this chapter: to be real is to lead with personal integrity. No leader will last long without it. But what does it mean to be real, i.e., to have integrity—and how do we apply this to equip us to become pro leaders?

Keeping It Real

A principle I wrote down on the legal pad I kept in my top desk drawer was "To be real is to lead with personal integrity." No leader will be able to build a following in the long term unless he or she can demonstrate personal integrity. As we move on in this next section, *Building Your Following*, we will pivot our view. We will change our perspective from an outward look to an inward one. We will turn once more to a great truth of leadership development: you must always excavate before you elevate. As Henry James so famously said, at the end of the day you must be able to say, "This is the real me." This is the root of personal integrity, what I believe to be the supreme quality of leadership.

To apply this principle, start by asking yourself a simple question: *As I lead, am I being true to myself?* If you have done the work to answer the two questions from the section on building your credibility (*Who am I?* and *What is my why?*)

the answer will be straightforward. But why ask the question? Because being true to yourself is not a thing you do once; rather it is a daily habit requiring consistent application of discipline over time.

Much of leadership is learned on the job, and as a new or a young leader it is common to look to emulate other leaders. The problem comes when what started as *emulation* becomes *imitation,* resulting in losing yourself in the process. Where this happens, a positive—emulation—turns into a negative—imitation. **That is why it is so important to check yourself and be certain your leadership is springing from the real you.** If it's not, you will have problems. But here's the good news: correcting those problems will require nothing more than getting back to the real you.

Let me give a personal illustration. I am Midwest born and bred, so when we combined our company with one headquartered in New York, and I became the leader of the combined company, my Midwestern style was immediately challenged. Combining two cultures—Midwest and East Coast—was a challenge, a big test of my own leadership skills. At first, I tried to carry on two styles of leadership, one for Minneapolis and one for New York. The only problem was it did not work—I am not a New Yorker, and no matter what I did, it never felt natural. I encountered a number of gifted leaders in my time in New York, and while there was much in them worth emulating, I failed at imitation; it just wasn't me.

I will never forget the day I came to the realization that I was trying to be something I was not. I was in a session with my executive coach, Bill Berman, discussing a leadership struggle I was having. After listening to me for a while, he said, "It sounds like you just need to be yourself." He was right!

I stepped back, looked at the issue, saw where I was not leading in a way that was true to myself, made the adjustment, and very quickly the matter self-corrected.

I've found that there are three ways to stay real:

1. Be true to yourself: be authentic.
2. Be honest.
3. Be vulnerable.

Being authentic is the easiest way to be yourself—you simply leave your mask off, and you allow people to see you just as you are; you're *genuine*. Next, being honest is demonstrating the attribute of being simple or unpretentious. Do not fear coming across as unsophisticated; it can actually be an attractive quality. Think of Abraham Lincoln; from all I have studied of his life, he did not have one ounce of pretension. And third, embrace vulnerability as another way to keep yourself real. When vulnerability is applied with both discernment and discretion, it can be a powerful and attractive force of your leadership.

In my coaching practice, vulnerability is an attribute I see most leaders run from at almost any cost, believing that showing any type of vulnerability will cause the people they lead to see them as weak. Most learned the hard way that vulnerability often hurt them as they moved upward. But I propose that, on the contrary, to demonstrate appropriate vulnerability to your team is a powerful psychological motivator because it allows your followers to relate to you as human. Because of this, they will be drawn to you. Humility is an admired quality that enables people to be vulnerable.

Authenticity, honesty, and vulnerability are powerful leadership tools. If you cultivate these three attributes in your life and your leadership, it will keep you real and assure you are being true to yourself. This in turn will grow your following.

The Power of Vulnerability

I experienced the power of appropriate vulnerability when I was once asked to speak to a gathering of five hundred business leaders. In my preparation, I asked the leader of the group for some advice. Twenty years my senior, he was an icon of the community. I was expecting sage advice on the specifics of my talk. Instead, he was short and to the point when he said, "Unless you are willing to 'drop tough,' don't step up there." When I looked quizzically at him, he said, "You need to be real—honest. Take your mask off; that's true leadership." So, I did, and although I was more nervous than I normally would have been, it was effective. To my great surprise, the reaction from the group I spoke to was greater than I had ever experienced before. Twenty-five years later, I still occasionally will run into someone who heard me speak that day, and they will often cite a point of vulnerability they found encouraging. I've never forgotten that experience.

Why is being vulnerable a powerful leadership tactic? All human beings struggle with some form of insecurity or self-doubt; if you need convincing of this, just read M. Scott Peck's work *The Road Less Traveled*. Since this is true, when you as a leader are vulnerable about your-own insecurities and self-doubt, it will form a connection between you and your followers at an innate level that can help them feel safe to be vulnerable with you. For example, whenever I speak to a new group, I admit my nervousness around public speaking. It has been proven the average person fears public speaking more than death. Therefore, my admission usually triggers a sympathetic reaction, which draws them closer to me as the speaker. The same is true in leadership; if you open yourself up, chances are your followers will open up, too.

Two risks are paramount when being vulnerable as a leader; these are lack of discernment and lack of discretion. As a leader, you must always be discerning, and you must always be discreet. Fail with one or both, and your leadership effort will suffer because you will lose followers—either mentally, emotionally, or physically.

What I mean by "discernment" is this: as a leader, you must be able to read your followers, being able to understand where they are mentally and emotionally. How much and what information is appropriate to share? The answer will be different based on their relation to your "inner circle."

Let me give you a practical example. When I founded my company, we were a true start-up, and, like most entrepreneurial businesses, things ran pretty lean in the early days. We counted every penny, and, as my wife so aptly put it, "We always had cake, but not always frosting." Yet, we did not share our financial facts with our children. To do so would not have been fair to them, since they had no way to affect or control the circumstances. In a similar manner, when leading an organization, it is important the leader doesn't place undue pressure on associates who have little or no ability to affect the outcome.

Here is a real-life personal experience that demonstrates discernment:

My CFO to me: "Andy, if our client doesn't pay us this week as promised, we won't be able to cover payroll."

Me to my CFO: "Thank you, I will make a call."

Later that day, an associate to me: "You look stressed, is there anything I can do?"

My response: "Thank you for asking. I don't mean to pass my stress on to you, I am simply feeling my responsibility to you and the rest of our team, and the best way for you to help me is to continue to do the great job you have been doing."

That associate went back to her work, believing that I cared for her. But had I told her I was stressed about making payroll, instead of being able to focus on her work, she would have worried that she wasn't going to get paid and all that goes with that. In her position, she had no way to affect accounts receivable, so telling her the whole truth would have been unfair to her. The rest of the story: I called the client and they paid their invoice and gave us some additional work, too.

Closely related to discernment is discretion. Although vulnerability is a powerful tool of leadership, it must be exercised with discretion, which is a learned character trait vital to effective leadership. Too much information ("TMI") is a common phrase today. Sharing too much information—i.e., being too detailed or specific with the wrong audience or at the wrong time—can do more harm than good and can distract your leadership efforts.

I learned to be discreet the hard way: by being indiscreet. As a young associate, I was having lunch at a downtown restaurant known as a power lunch spot. There, I boasted to my lunch mate about a client I had been able to bring to the firm. Little did I know, at the table next to me was a friend of our CEO. When I returned to the office, I had a message to see the CEO, ASAP. His friend had called him and shared my indiscretion. I will spare you the details of a very uncomfortable meeting with my boss, but it was the best lesson on being discreet that I could have ever learned. I encourage you to learn from my mistake: when opening yourself up to others and being real, be careful what you say to whom, and think before you speak.

Being real is having personal integrity and integrity is the supreme quality of leadership. Without it, you will have a difficult time building a following, but with it, your leadership will create a following.

Next, we will continue on the theme of excavating before elevating, looking at another key ability every pro leader must possess—the ability to lead *yourself.* That is the focus of our next chapter.

Principle Application

1. Are you the same person at the office and at home?

2. Is there something you wish you could say to someone that you're not currently saying?

3. If you could have a do-over, what would it be?

4. How would you define integrity?

11 | First, Lead Yourself

"You cannot lead others until you have
first learned to lead yourself."
—Robin S. Sharma

PRO LEADERSHIP PRINCIPLE: I am the most
important person I will ever lead.

When it comes to coaching leaders—whether they are founding entrepreneurs, growth company CEOs, or other senior
leaders—experience has taught me they all have learned one
truth: it's lonely at the top. That is one reason having a coach
is so valuable.

But a coach is not enough. I always recommend my clients have at least two additional people as part of their inner
support circle: a PGA teaching pro and a therapist. (If golf is
not your thing, then find the "pro" instructor in whatever your
thing is and take some lessons.) But by all means, I hope you
will find yourself a therapist you are comfortable with, one
with whom you can talk openly and bring your true self.

Why? Advances in psychology indicate that nothing beats
therapy in helping to re-wire circled thinking. We all have
implicit memories that influence our behavior, and it is now

understood these memories reside in our right brains, and our left brain is not capable of sorting out our right brain. To accomplish this, we need someone else's right brain—enter your coach, your therapist, your partner, et al.

I didn't just read this; I have learned it is true. Let me share how. When I came to the conclusion that closing the doors of the business I founded, loved, and had labored in for nearly twenty-three years was the best choice for me and all of my associates, I needed someone to talk to about it. This was a clear case of being lonely at the top, i.e., my role required me to make a decision that would affect the lives of many people. But discernment and discretion required that I not process this decision openly with my team, so I called my therapist.

I left a voicemail. "I would like to get on your calendar. I would like your help processing something." A few days later, I sat in her office and quietly related to her what had been going on in my life the past eighteen months. I shared with her all of my innermost anxieties, feelings, and insecurities. (I trust her completely; she is a wonderful person and a gifted therapist.)

I was heartbroken that the business would come to an end. I felt like I had failed not only myself, but my team and all those who had put so much trust in me. My thoughts were circling in my mind and I couldn't break the cycle without another "right brain" to help me process and turn a negative into a positive. My healing over this heartbreak began in her office that day. I needed to lead others through the process that would ensue when I announced my decision. But the first person I needed to lead through it was myself.

The Process of Self-Leadership

The process of self-leadership is a cycle that contains several steps. I have identified seven here that I've come to realize are required of me as I lead myself. You may identify others that help you. The important thing is to keep in mind is that it is a cycle, and it is daily. Some days you may need to apply the process multiple times. That is normal; after all, we are not robots.

Here is my seven-factor process of self-leadership, step by step:

1. Destination
2. WIN
3. Motivation
4. Inspiration
5. Do it now
6. Follow your process
7. Have fun and enjoy your life

First, start with your destination. Where do you want to go and why? Review the work you did earlier on knowing yourself and knowing your why. My why, my primary governing belief, and my mission occupy the header of my daily digital planner. Because of their importance, I review them at least once each day. This discipline will remind you where you are going and help you from being distracted by the many things that compete for your attention each day. Many things will seem urgent, but they are not important. As Stephen Covey so aptly taught, begin with the end in mind so that the urgent does not keep you from the important.

Second, identify your most important things for the day. WIN is an acronym I use for What's Important Now. I have learned that my to-do or task capacity is limited to no more than five each day. My daily "WIN 5" is the list of my five most important tasks for that day. WIN 5 works for me, daily and weekly.

Take time each week to answer the question, "In the next week, what are the five most important tasks I need to accomplish if I am to be where I want to be at this time next week?" Then at the end of each day, review and make your WIN 5 plan for the next day.

Third, review what motivates you. Reviewing your why may be all you need, but there may be additional motivations. For example, when I was a kid I wanted a ten-speed bike. I found the one I wanted, and the bike shop let me put it on layaway. Each week I brought them twenty dollars, and ten weeks later I rode the bike home. My desire for the bike motivated me to get up each summer morning at 5:30 a.m. to caddy as often as I could to earn the money to get that bike. What motivates you?

Next, step four, identify what inspires you. Music, poetry, reading, exercise? What charges your batteries? Whatever it is, do it daily. You will never inspire others unless and until you have been inspired yourself.

Step five: do it now. Do it now, do it now. (Did I mention you should do it now?) Refuse to procrastinate. Stop planning—execute. Remember, beginning is half done.

Step six: follow a process to get your task done. Dr. Morris Pickens is a sports psychologist who is famous in golf circles for the help he has given to many PGA Tour players, several of whom have won major championships. Pickens has a discipline he teaches his clients and he has written about it in his book, *The Winning Way in Golf and Life*. Since reading Pickens' book, I have adopted his process, and it has benefited me not only on the golf course, but in all other areas of my life, too. Here it is: Pickens understands 85 percent of a golfer's success is mental. In this sport—and in any other endeavor— managing your mind is critical to success.

Pickens has developed a four-step process to help his clients accomplish this mental discipline: Refocus, Routine, Reflex, Relax. It goes like this: As you are walking up to your ball, when you are ten paces away you refocus, you come back into your game, and you think about the shot you need to make and where you want the ball to end up. Once you have determined this, you move into your pre-shot routine.

This is a routine you never vary from; you repeat it for every shot. Now, you stop thinking about the shot and you allow your reflexes to execute the shot you have hit countless times before. Following the shot, you relax, you enjoy the walk, and you don't think about the next shot or anything golf related until you are ten paces away from your ball. Then you start the process all over again: Refocus, Routine, Reflex, Relax. Repeat, repeat, repeat, until you are finished.

Application has taught me this process is not only effective on the golf course; it is effective in the writer's studio, and in the executive suite, and on the factory floor. Think of how you could apply this to your own self-leadership. It has worked for me and I'm confident it will work for you, too.

Finally, have some fun; enjoy your life and what you are doing. If you don't or you can't, hit the pause button and figure it out. Talk it through with someone--your coach, your therapist, your partner, or your friend. If you are working at your highest and best, you will be fed by it and it will energize you. It will also be fun—more times than not!

The Discipline of Self-Leadership

I emphasize the need to take time for fun in all this because it is doubtful there is a greater challenge you will confront as a leader than self-leadership. Succeed in this and you will have gone a long way down the road of pro leadership. To win this battle, you will need to make self-leadership a disciplined daily habit. If it were all work and no fun, that would be drudgery indeed! That being said, though, self-leadership is a discipline and it's not always fun—or easy.

For me, self-leadership starts with my alarm at 5:15 a.m. each morning. I wake up undisciplined, and I spend the first hour of each day refocusing on who I am, my why, my mission, and my daily WIN 5. I end each day by spelling out my WIN 5 for the next day. I do not want to have to wake up in the morning and then plan how that day will be spent. A great leader ends his day by setting his priorities for the next.

Having that process in place set me up for the self-leadership required to write this book. Starting and writing a manuscript took all of the discipline I could muster and required all of my leadership skills; I was a tough person to lead. But, in the process of writing, this pro leadership principle—that I am the most important person I will ever lead—was proven to me all over again. And, over time, I became a better follower.

One of the things I mentioned to my therapist while working through the closure of my company was my list of lessons I had learned in my career—a list I kept in the top drawer of my desk. I happened to have it with me that day she was helping me process the experience. She asked me a question and I answered with a lesson I had learned. "That would be lesson #27," I said, quoting to her the single sentence that represented the leadership principle I had written down. She asked me what I meant by lesson #27, and I shared my list with her— there were twenty-nine lessons on the list that day. (I have since added a few more. Leaders are never done learning.)

"That sounds like it would be a good book—twenty-nine lessons, twenty-nine chapters. I think you should write it," she said. I laughed, but admitted I had always wanted to write; however, I thought no one needs another book on leadership. She told me she did not think that was true. "Perhaps," she said thoughtfully, "your experiences could help others."

"Okay," I replied, "I'll consider it." This book came from that list I shared with my therapist—with a great deal of help from my wonderful team and exercising the pro leadership principle of self-leadership.

Applying Self-Leadership to New Processes

The writing process has taught me that being an author is another expression of my calling as an entrepreneur. After all, a book starts with an idea, leads to a vision and a strategy, follows the process and procedures of writing, and its author implements tactical skills to accomplish the mission. An author is required to believe in something first, before anyone else does.

You fight opposition—from within and without. You learn perseverance—how to fight your way through to the end. The whole process is creative and necessitates growth. It reminds me of what King Solomon said, "All work leads to a profit, but mere talk leads to poverty." You learn so many lessons along the way: you learn to be discreet, to keep your tongue, to work by yourself, and to fight through resistance. I had to face myself so I could know myself. And I learned things along the way. I had to lead myself (in the writing process), before I could lead others (through what I would write in my book).

So, I led myself through the creative process. I am a morning person; I am most creative then. When I figured out I needed to write when I was most creative, I set my alarm and got up to write. I also learned I can focus for about ninety minutes at a time, and I am able to write about 1,250 words in ninety minutes. I learned I cannot write more than I have read—reading is an author's fuel—so I read every day.

I learned to prepare the next day's writing the day before—just a rough outline, a central idea or principle, a rough sketch. I was also fortunate to gain the friendship of a pro leader who was also a pro author.

I was also helped by the memory of another pro author I knew. A few years before he died, I got to know Vince Flynn. Vince was a great guy who became a "big league" fiction author. Once, when we were together, I asked him how he wrote books. "Three pages a day," was his answer, "Three hundred and fifty words per page, and that means 1,050 words a day." He also quoted an unknown author who said, "I only write when I am inspired, and I make sure I am inspired every day at 9:30." I took those words to heart.

My family and I spent time in a cabin neighboring the one Vince used as his writer's studio. We were there for three summers as Vince completed one of his Mitch Rapp novels. We all knew not to interrupt his work between 9:30 a.m. and noon; three pages were being written. I admired his discipline and self-leadership—he was a pro! And he was a great example to me.

In summary, whether they are executives, entrepreneurs, or authors (or all three or anything else), pro leaders know they are the most important person they will ever lead, and they have a plan for doing it effectively. So, the takeaway is knowing yourself well enough to know how to set yourself up for success. If you need a plan, or maybe just a fresh approach, I encourage you to use the one I've provided as a template. Then, over time, you can adjust it to your own personal style, and then it will become your own. You will know it is when you find yourself teaching it to someone else.

Remember, without leadership nothing happens, strong, caring servant leadership is good leadership, and good leadership produces good results. So, be a good leader and start with yourself!

Principle Application

1. What grade would you give your self-leadership? Why?

2. What does a balanced life look like to you?

3. Are you living that life now? Why or why not?

4. What steps could you take to build or protect that balance?

5. What is one thing you could change to improve your self-leadership?

12 | Praise in Public, Correct in Private

"I have often regretted my speech, never my silence."
—Publilius Syrus

> **PRO LEADERSHIP PRINCIPLE:** All a leader's words have influence, so choose them wisely.

"Words are like toothpaste," she said to me. "Once they come out of your mouth you can never put them back."

Little did I know this simple saying was a profound truth that one day would have a huge impact on my leadership. Through it, I learned another important principle of pro leadership: All a leader's words have influence so choose them wisely. Yes, what we say and how we say it really matters; in fact, in this digital age defined by social media, where so little of our interaction is face to face, the spoken word has more gravity today than ever.

And who was the wise woman who uttered those words to me, the one who imparted to me this simple but transforming truth? The answer is a story.

A young associate, quickly climbing the ladder at a nationally known asset management firm, was responsible for the regional rollout of a start-up mutual fund family. However, he was in over his head. He had been given too much responsibility too soon. In addition, he lacked the authority to match his responsibility. Ask him today and he would tell you his biggest deficiency was character, resulting in poor judgment. He was, however, good with words; he could be clever and bitingly sarcastic. But those words lacked wisdom. Add to this a leaning toward perfectionism and what you had were all the ingredients of a poor leader.

As the date of the planned roll-out approached, the pressure mounted, and this poor leader's true colors began to show themselves. Several dozen associates made up the operations team he led and were vital to a successful rollout. Hundreds of tasks were required to be completed accurately for the mission to succeed. The weak link was the people. Few had ever been a part of a rollout such as this, but neither had their leader.

A mistake was made, which caused him to look bad. He handled it, or so he thought—in public, with an audience of nearly three dozen members of the operations team—by chastising and berating his associate for her stupid mistake. She was mortified; anyone would have been. But the young leader overplayed his hand. He showed his own arrogance and inexperience as he marched proudly back into his office, leaving relational wreckage in his wake. He returned to his task list, believing he had solved his problem. After all, he had a deadline to meet, and sometimes, he thought, the ends justify the means.

Five minutes later, he was interrupted by a call from the executive assistant to his boss's boss. "He wants to see you NOW!" The next quarter hour of our young leader's life was an uncomfortable but transforming lesson he would never forget.

"You have a lot of skills, but your tongue will kill them all if you aren't careful," the CEO told him. "How you handled this situation was wrong, and I won't tolerate this type of behavior around here."

The young leader was given a new assignment, beginning with the woman he had publicly chastised; he was to apologize to her. Then he was to go to each of the associates on the operations team and apologize to them, one at a time.

That is what I did, and it was a lesson I will never forget—I don't think any leadership lesson has had a greater impact on my leadership than this one did. And the woman who spoke the words to me, "Words are like toothpaste; once they come out of your mouth you can never put them back," she was the woman I had publicly humiliated, the first woman I apologized to. She was twenty years my senior, and had been a loyal member of the firm for longer than I had been alive. The good news is, I learned a great lesson, and she became a trusted ally for as long as we worked together. I will never forget her, or the lesson she helped me learn.

Throughout this book, I have related many personal experiences, but this one may be the one I consider the most personally impactful. Certainly, the experience is seared in my memory. I will never forget the personal humiliation of having to apologize to thirty-six individuals, one at a time. Looking back, I am grateful for the experience, and that my mentor and boss saw enough in me to teach me and help me grow. Had I been in his shoes, I am not sure I would have been so gracious and forgiving. The good news is, as I have led teams since then, I have had countless opportunities to follow his example. Only a few times have I found an individual not worthy of the second chance I gave them, but in the vast majority of cases, a second chance was the right thing to do.

A Better Way to Communicate

Let's walk together through the process of analysis and assessment I would use today, if I found myself in a similar position. It is a three-question review developed by my friend and executive coach, Jay Coughlan. He developed this process as a CEO in the software industry, and he wrote about it in his book, *Five Bold Choices*. Few tools have provided me greater help in assessing and analyzing outcomes, and in breaking the decision-making log jams so common in leadership. The three questions are:

- What did I (or we) do right?
- In hindsight what would I (or we) do differently?
- What am I (or we) going to change?

First, what did I do right? Most leaders, when assessing an outcome, start with a negative: what did we do wrong? Doing so naturally results in a defensive posture for you and your team. No one wants to be wrong and no one wants to look bad. As a result of beginning an assessment with a negative, it will often be harder to get to the truth, slowing the overall process and restricting relational and team growth. On the other hand, beginning with a positive has the effect of lowering defenses and getting to the truth quicker.

Second, in hindsight, what would I do differently? This question allows you to take what you have learned and apply that wisdom to this experience. As the wisdom of the ages goes, hindsight is 20:20. I agree, with one addendum: hindsight is 20:20 only if you learn from it and apply it to your leadership.

In hindsight, how could my example of amateur leadership be turned into an example of pro leadership? In my case, it would have been by remembering a simple relational truth: when dealing with people, praise in public, but correct in private. I corrected in public, hurting the person and damaging relationships. The action resulted in an increase in work, and a degrading of my team when the opposite was needed. Not only that, but my tone was wrong. King Solomon wrote, "A gentle answer deflects anger, but harsh words make tempers flare." Had I confronted this error kindly and gently, I know this person would have accepted responsibility. Her mistake was not intentional, just a common human error. A pro leader will help a team member to learn and grow from such an error and, as a result, help them become a stronger member of the team.

Thirdly, what am I going to change? There may be several things, in reflection, you would do differently, but it is not in your power to change all of those things. It is another leadership truth that we should only focus on the things we can affect. Too much leadership emotional energy is wasted when we focus on things over which we have no control. Wrestling only with the things you can actually affect is life giving to a leader. Leaders are inherently people of action, so when you consider what you are going to change, limit your mental energy to only those things you really do have control over or can influence.

Back to my example—what would I change? That's simple. I would have been more humble and self-aware from the beginning, and more courageous in standing up for myself and my team when we were assigned the project. We were moving too fast, because I had accepted a timetable that was unrealistic, and I did not have the courage of leadership to stand up to those who had set the goal for us. So, when the inevitable mistake was made, my frustration came out sideways and I "lost it" on a valuable team member when the true fault was mine, not hers. Another thing I would do differently would be, in the moment of frustration, hit the pause button, go for a walk, and consider how best to handle the matter so I would not adversely affect the individual, the team, or our mission.

Good leadership improves every situation it steps into, and is able to correct and encourage the team and its members in a way that fosters relationships. The easiest way to ensure this happens is to understand the influence you have because of your position as leader and choose your words wisely.

In the years since I learned the above lesson on "tongue management," I have had ample opportunities to repeat my folly, but haven't. Instead I have adopted several communication principles that help me manage the tension that is so much a part of good communication. I hesitate to give a list, because it is human nature to take a list and turn it into "rules." And if you take this list as rules you will miss the point. This is a list of principles. There is a difference: rules change, principles do not. It is often difficult to separate the rule from the exception, but a principle can be adapted to fit the changing circumstances of your leadership.

Principles of Wise Words, Wisely Spoken

Wise words are the direct result of the combined application of several other relational and communication principles:

1. Good leaders first listen, then reflect, next clarify, and finally encourage.
2. Good leaders must be builders (of people).
3. Criticism is never constructive.
4. Sarcasm is an ineffective leadership tool.

Let's consider these principles and how they help leaders guard their tongues, and, in the end, their influence.

The art of listening is a vital characteristic of leadership. **The principle is this: good leaders first listen, then reflect, next clarify, and finally encourage.** This principle helps a leader to guard his or her tongue by slowing down and extending the communication process.

A friend of mine sent me a photo of a plaque she saw hanging in a small town gift store, which said, "I don't like to think before I speak, I like to be just as surprised as everyone else by what comes out of my mouth." Her text, sent with a smiling emoji, said, "After I thought of myself when I saw this, I thought of you."

I texted back, "Too true, and I cannot wait to use this." Like Publilius, quoted at the opening of this chapter, I have often regretted my words but never my silence. Stephen Covey taught that a leader must always seek first to understand, before being understood. This is a prescription to listen first. If we listen first, we will not only gain understanding, but we will gain the time needed to formulate an appropriate response. Then, by reflecting what they have said back to the person we are engaged with, we increase our understanding.

To gain even greater understanding, we may ask a clarifying question or two. These steps alone will go a long way to assure your response is productive. But if you add an encouraging word at the end of each response, you are accomplishing the added benefit of building up the one you are relating to.

I would add along with this point that leaders should not only listen first, but they should speak last. I don't mean that leaders should have the last word; to practice that is not only unwise, but it is poor relational form. But, to speak last is a wise and powerful leadership strategy. Simply, it is a matter of timing.

As the leader, your team will naturally be influenced by your opinion—so much so, that if you speak before your team members have spoken, they may not be as forthcoming in giving their opinions if they don't agree with you. So, by speaking last, you will assure you have had the benefit of the whole team's opinions. (This is a small example of "leadership from the backseat," which is the subject of the next chapter.)

The second supporting principle of guarding your tongue is that good leaders are builders (of people). There is enough in this world that weighs people down; do not allow your leadership to add to the burden the members of your team are already carrying. Every day we have a choice about how to use the words that will leave our mouths each day: we can use them to tear people down, or build them up. A kind, gentle and encouraging word, given in the right tone, is an easy way to build your team. It doesn't cost anything to be nice!

The next principle to remember when guarding your tongue is that criticism is never constructive. Recent strides in understanding the psychology of the human mind has proven the damage caused by criticism and how it creates implicit memories that can negatively affect human performance long after the issue resulting in the criticism has passed. Criticism is destructive and harmful to relationships and to team building. A pro leader doesn't criticize, rather he or she coaches and encourages, all the while with the goal of developing the team through positive actions. Pro leaders coach; they don't criticize. Rather than finding fault, ask questions such as, "Help me understand why?" or, "What is it you were hoping to accomplish?" Asking questions with a positive tone is an effective coaching method.

The final supporting principle to guarding our tongues is that sarcasm is an ineffective leadership tool. Men are notorious for being sarcastic, and I am a pro at it myself. But I have learned it is a poor tool in the hands of a leader, and, as a result, I have removed it permanently from my toolbox. I now challenge those I coach to consider its effectiveness.

The origin of the word "sarcasm" comes from the Greek word *sarkazein,* which literally means "to tear or strip the flesh off." Sarcasm is often referred to as "cutting," and no wonder—it can really hurt! As witty as sarcasm may feel in the moment, it is actually hostility disguised as humor. Though they may smile and play along outwardly, those on the receiving end of sarcastic comments often feel diminished and even humiliated. A better practice is to consider before speaking, *Do the words I intend to speak edify, unify, and fortify, the person and mission I am leading?* If the answer to any of these is no, then you'd best guard your tongue.

In every area of my life—husband, father, grandfather, neighbor, and more—I know my words influence and impact the people around me. In my role as coach, saying the wrong thing, even in jest, could hinder a client in the transformation they desire and have asked me to help them achieve. So, I try to be careful with not only *what* I say, but *how* I say it. When coaching leaders, I follow a simple discussion pattern: listen, reflect, ask, repeat. Listen to what is being said, and reflect it back to them so they may hear what they said, and clarify any misconceptions. Next, ask a clarifying question or two, until you understand completely what they are saying. Once you understand, you are in a position to be understood. If you take the time to do this, there is a good chance that your words that follow will be wise and constructive to you, your associates, and the mission you are leading.

─────────── **Principle Application** ───────────

1. Consider a recent personal leadership interaction in which you had to bring correction to someone:

    • What did you do right?

    • What would you do differently if you could do it again?

2. In your leadership how is your balance between praise and correction? Do you tend toward one or the other?

3. How has that balance affected your leadership?

13 | Be Willing to Take a Back Seat

"The growth and development of people is
the highest calling of leadership."
—Harvey S. Firestone

> **PRO LEADERSHIP PRINCIPLE:** Leadership development is done best from the back seat.

For five years, our company had an office in New York City, and when I was there, I spent a lot of time being driven around—to and from the airport, to and from the office, and all around the city. The advent of Uber was awesome! I have a pretty good Uber rating—not perfect, but good enough that most of the time, I get a ride quickly.

On the other hand, I had a few associates whose ratings often meant that we might not get a ride in a timely manner. They weren't bad people; it's just that they didn't like the back seat! Many of them often started a ride by telling the Uber driver which way he should go and concluded by critiquing his driving techniques during the trip. At the end of each trip they would rate the driver, and the driver would rate them. (Kind of an object lesson in living by the sword and dying by it!)

Those experiences were the seed of the "back seat principle" for me. Use your imagination here: when you get into the back seat of a car, you are not driving. You are not in control; you have turned the execution of your journey over to someone else. From the back seat, you may enjoy the ride, join the conversation, encourage the driver, or offer direction, if asked.

Getting in the back seat, figuratively speaking, is a coaching and a leadership discipline. It is an idea, a way of thinking, a way of leading—an effective practice good for relationships and quality leadership. Getting out of the driver's seat and into the "back seat" is also a way of nurturing a positive, productive relationship, because it can be transformative in many ways. I have found it to be a foundational principle not only of my life in general, but also of my leadership consulting company.

Leadership by Invitation

Although the back seat principle came to me literally in the back seat of an Uber, the principle was reinforced by my parenting role as I transitioned my relationships with my three adult children, who are now all well established and growing into what and whom they were created to be. I love and am proud of each of them but, more importantly, I *like* them. They are fun to be around. As adults, they have their own lives, which don't always include Mom and Dad. We have transitioned in our parenting to an "invitation-only" involvement. We invite them, and they invite us, and "no" is always an acceptable answer; we respect "no." This has resulted in good boundaries all around.

We have learned that when we are invited into their lives, we must be willing to sit in the back seat, because if we insist on driving or otherwise being in control, we won't get invited as often. But, if we are willing to give up control, invitations will come, and that will give us an opportunity to share our wisdom and influence them for good.

The same is true in most relationships in life, be they personal or business. Good leadership is by invitation only. It is not heavy handed or dictatorial, it does its best work from the backseat, it maintains good boundaries, and it respects a "no."

How can I say that good leadership is by invitation only? Simple. To be a successful leader is to *inspire* your followers to come along—to buy into the vision you have laid out and the strategic plan that was born from your vision. Followers will only follow for so long because they have to, because their job depends on it. But in the long run, if they don't believe from the inside out, they will drop out. At best, they will look like a follower, but their heart isn't in it. They are not motivated to bring their best and, as a result, are often ineffective. In the end, we see that, time and time again, effective leadership invites, while mere management demands.

Good leadership is humble, and respects a no. If a follower says no, either in words or in deeds, it is the job of the leader to hear, to see, and to respect it. I'm not saying the leader has to accept the no, but it does mean you have to slow down, because a no means you have some more work to do before moving forward. Leaders need to *understand* a no, to start with why, and then listen and understand. Sometimes a no is actually good for leadership!

Leaders vs. Managers

The back seat principle is counter-intuitive. "Leadership by invitation," and "understanding the no" are not the kinds of principles we generally think of first when we think of leaders, but we should. One reason we don't is because we often confuse leadership with management.

Not all managers are leaders and not all leaders are managers, although all leaders are responsible for management. Can you see the difference? I have witnessed high-level leaders who were incapable of management; but they knew it, so they surrounded themselves with strong managers. It is the application of the 80:20 principle: do what you do best and hire the rest. My strengths are leadership, not management, so I have learned whatever mission I am on to have a strong manager at my right hand. Yet, not all managers are leaders; a pro leader is able to see the difference.

Several years ago, I was sharing with a mentor a business struggle I was having. "Well," he said, "I think the best thing for you to do is move to the wisdom seat." I was confused. He could see it on my face and hear it in my voice.

After a few moments' pause to ensure I was paying attention, he replied, "Sometimes the best thing a leader can do is turn the wheel over to his leaders, because often it is the only way they will learn and grow. You need the wisdom to know when the time is right." The back seat principle precisely embodies this philosophy.

The back seat is the wisdom seat I was referring to, and the application of the back seat principle requires a leader to know the answer to four questions:

1. Can I lead without driving?
2. How's my driving?
3. How do I know it is time to move to the back seat?
4. What happens if I don't move back?

It never takes long in a new coaching relationship to get to the back seat principle of leadership, because it is so vital to the development of a leadership team. I find whenever I proclaim this principle—that leadership development is done best from the backseat—the first thing I hear is often a respectful chuckle. Or, I might receive a quizzical look, immediately followed by a request to clarify or, depending on the personality of the one I am coaching, a laugh out loud and a quick, "You have got to be kidding!" response.

Like my former mentor, I have learned to pause for effect, then look them straight in the eye and respond, "I'm dead serious." Then I wait while silence does its work. Normally there is subsequently a toned-down response, such as, "I thought I couldn't lead unless I drove." Here is where the paradigm shift occurs; *you don't need to drive in order to lead.*

Driving as a metaphor for leading is a helpful way for many leaders to understand and to apply leadership principles—men, generally speaking, especially benefit because cars are so much a part of our lives. In fact, in my experience, leaders who are also women often grasp the benefits of leadership from the back seat more easily than do leaders who are men. Why? My youngest daughter answered the question for me, saying, "Dad, dudes need to drive; it's how they are."

With men, I am reminded of one of my favorite scenes from that great comedy *Talladega Nights,* where Ricky

Bobby, played by Will Ferrell, is discussing a race with his friend Cal Naughton Jr., played by John C. Reilly. In the scene, Cal tells Ricky he would like him to let him win a race, to which Ricky replies, "But, if I let you win, how can I win?" Like Ricky Bobby, when my mentor counseled me move to the backseat (wisdom seat), I responded, "How can I lead from there?" True, it is a paradoxical principle, but the truth is that leadership from the back seat is doubly effective. It not only furthers the mission, but also develops leaders in the process. It does so by giving them the authority and responsibility of driving.

Knowing When It's Time to Drive (or Not)

However, sometimes as a leader, you are required to drive. Consider times when you have led your organization down a new and unproven path. In times like these, the leader is best behind the wheel, because often he or she is the one with the vision and the necessary skill to see beyond the headlights. In cases such as this, the right question is to ask, "How's my driving?" Again, this is a question of excavation before elevation— it is about leadership self-evaluation. To take the metaphor another step, I might ask, "How is the ride for those who are in the car with you? Is it smooth or bumpy? Would you like to be your own passenger?"

I remember a time I was asked to speak on a Big Ten campus to a group of students. It was a five-hour drive from my home, but my schedule did not allow time for driving, so a friend and accomplished pilot offered to fly me in his Cessna 210. He was a highly experienced pilot, so I quickly agreed. Four others who expressed an interested in coming along joined us. On the flight out, I sat in the right front seat, thrilled to be there for my first ever cockpit experience.

After we had taken off, Captain Dan asked me if I would like to fly the plane. I did, and after a few instructions on how to keep it level, he let me take the yoke. Flying for the first time was a thrill, and I considered myself an excellent rookie pilot—that is, until I looked back at the four souls seated behind me; all were various shades of green. Apparently, I had been bouncing us around quite a bit and my passengers were suffering for it. Very graciously, Dan took the plane back, and the ride smoothed back out, as did the passengers' stomachs.

Leadership is like that. If you are driving, you must know the ride you are giving your team. Hopefully, you are able to look around and see how they are feeling. If you cannot, it is a question for your inner circle, those who are willing to speak truth to you.

Apart from the times circumstances require you to drive, how do you know it is time to move from the driver's seat into the back seat? This is where discernment comes in. Remember the wisdom pyramid of a couple of chapters ago: from a base of experience comes judgment, which is followed by wisdom. The more leadership experience you have, the better able you will be to judge whether or not it is time for a leader you are developing to drive. This is a one-on-one decision; not every young leader will be ready for added responsibility at the same time.

Some signs that it is time for you to move to the back seat and allow your leaders to drive are:

1. **They have bought into the mission's vision and have taken *Extreme Ownership*,** as former Navy

Seals Jocko Willink and Leif Babin wrote about in their leadership book by the same name. No one is ready to lead unless they accept responsibility for a mission and then take responsibility for the results.

2. **They have faced failure and handled it well**; they have learned from it, and it bent them but did not break them. I count as one of my greatest personal leadership lessons the experience(s) of giving leadership to individuals who have succeeded but never failed, only to watch them be broken by life's inevitable failures. So much of the world we live in is too ready to dismiss a leader due to failure when the truth is that failure is often the very qualifier and preamble to pro leadership. Clearly, there must be a level of competence equal to the responsibility. But, as leaders, we do ourselves, and our missions, a disservice if we make success the primary qualifier and failure the disqualifier of leadership.

As I have spent countless hours interviewing leaders from all walks of life, I have asked them all this question: when hiring people what is the most important characteristic you look for? Those who I consider level-five leaders have all answered something along the same lines as this list: character, integrity, brokenness, and handling failure. Agreed. When looking for or developing leaders, when these boxes are checked, it is time to let them drive and for you to move to the back seat. You will accomplish your mission faster if you do.

This leads to the another important question I'm frequently asked, either explicitly or implicitly: "What happens if I don't get in the back seat? My answer is this: **the biggest risk of not moving to the backseat when the time is right**

is the loss of talent. Natural leaders normally aspire to lead, so they will look for opportunities to do so. If you don't provide them with those opportunities they will look elsewhere. I have seen it happen countless times, and the result has always eventually meant slowed growth and missed opportunities. This is a common management mistake: sometimes managers do everything they can to keep a great employee in place to serve their own interests versus that of the enterprise. This is short-term thinking and usually the great employee will leave. We all need to grow and lots of managers (and parents) keep trying to hold on.

As a leader, like it or not, you are in the leadership development business. The best place to accomplish this, as counter intuitive as it may sound, is from the backseat. It is where pro leaders learn to enjoy the ride. Granted, you do give up control when you move there, and that leads us to our final exercise in excavation before elevation—leaving room for providence—which is the subject of our next chapter.

Principle Application

1. Where have you experienced "management" being confused with "leadership"?

2. Recall a leader you've known who needed to get into the backseat. What causes you to believe this is the case?

3. How do you feel when you are leading but not "driving"?

4. Can you describe a time that "giving away your power" helped your leadership?

14 | Leave Room for Providence

"Providence has its appointed hour for everything.
We cannot command results; we can only strive."
—Mahatma Gandhi

"He that takes truth for his guide, and duty for his end,
may safely trust to God's providence to lead him aright."
—Blaise Pascal

"We failed, but in the good providence of God,
apparent failure often proves a blessing. "
—Robert E. Lee

PRO LEADERSHIP PRINCIPLE: Leaders influence outcomes but cannot control them.

Leaving room for providence is the final step in the personal excavation necessary before elevating to build your following. However, more than any chapter in this book this is the most personal to me. In it, I want to tell you the story of my faith, and why it is so vital to my life and my leadership.

Coming to faith as I did was the single greatest paradigm shift in my life. It changed my lens and, as a result, my trajectory. It's how I am able to prioritize people over possessions and relationships over rules. My faith has also allowed me to find my calling, and to live in my essence. But, if a discussion of faith is not for you today, then move on and feel free to skip this chapter. You can pursue pro leadership without it, and if and when you are ready, it will be here.

My Ancestry DNA results put me at over 70 percent Anglo-Saxon with a heavy leaning toward Welsh. The results are not surprising. A number of years ago, before the fad of DNA testing came on the scene, *National Geographic* published an article on Wales. It was fascinating, but the best and most poignant part of it for me was the picture taken in a small Welsh town, a photograph of all its inhabitants. I couldn't help but notice that it could have been a family portrait with my brother and me standing in the front row!

Confirming my heritage has helped to answer a few curiosity questions, and it has helped to explain why I seem to be genetically predisposed in certain areas. However, when all is said and done, heritage is nice to know, not need to know. I am a futurist and not a historian, which means I care more about the future than the past. But we all have a story, and that story is the most important one you will ever tell. With that in mind, here's mine.

I am the youngest in a family of four children. I am thirteen years younger than my oldest sister, ten years younger than my next sister, and eight years younger than my brother. I was the family surprise. Born prematurely, I spent my first weeks on earth in an incubator in what would today be called a neonatal intensive care unit. The good news for me was the unique care I received as a result of the fact that my grandfather had been the pioneer of the practice of pediatric surgery on newborns and infants in the United States. The fortunate result of being his grandson was my being put under the 24/7 care of one of his many partners—all men whom he had personally mentored and trained (more about this later). As I look back, this was most certainly my first living experience of providence, since I have been told it is doubtful I would have survived without such tailor-made care.

As I was growing up in a middle-class neighborhood in Minneapolis and attending the same high school as my older siblings and my father had, there were three characteristics that won admiration in our home: academic or athletic achievement, and wealth. I learned early on that you are what you do and what you have. The fire of striving was stoked in me early.

Since my sisters were so much my senior, they were rarely present in my life, and I had little or no involvement in theirs. It was entirely different with my brother. He was the shining example, the one to emulate. I love him and am proud of him today, but apart from the fact that we look nearly identical, we are different people. We are separate and distinct personalities, which probably explains why we are able to enjoy each other now.

When I arrived at West High School as a freshman, a lot of positive anticipation preceded my arrival. In West High's history, up to that time, there had been only three athletes who had lettered twelve times—three sports in each of four years. My brother was the third and my father was the first. Although I loved athletics and desired to follow in both their footsteps, I did not possess the natural athletic abilities they did. This proved disappointing not only for me, but also for a few of the coaches I encountered. In fact, in the spring of my sophomore year, both the varsity football and hockey coach told me on separate occasions how disappointed they were I was not the athlete my brother had been. (I am not writing a book on psychology, but if I were, this would be in the chapter on what not to say to a teenager.)

Not only did my brother excel in athletics, but also in the classroom, where he was a straight-A student. This combination of academic and athletic ability earned him acceptance to Harvard to study and compete on their championship hockey team. It was exciting for him to have this opportunity and we were all proud to have him go there.

My father, a member of the greatest generation, did not attend college; rather he got his degree fighting in WWII on Normandy Beach and in the Pacific. He went back to college in 1946 and lasted only three weeks; he said he had learned too much in the war to sit and listen to professors who did not have the same experience he had. Today we know that he and so many others who fought so valiantly often suffered silently from untreated post-traumatic stress disorder (PTSD). My own study of PTSD and its causes and effects has helped me to have empathy toward my dad.

The difficult side of attending Harvard was the cost, and since they did not give athletic scholarships, my parents proudly bore the entire cost of my brother's education. That decision led to a difficult conversation between my father and me in the spring of my junior year at West. The expense of Harvard had been greater than they had anticipated and, as a result, there was little or no savings for my college. With tears running down his cheeks, he said they would help if they could, but I was going to be largely on my own, so I should plan on working my way through if I wanted to go.

Thanks to a reciprocal agreement between Minnesota and Wisconsin, I learned I could attend the UW Madison for the same tuition as the University of Minnesota. The combination of feeling I could never measure up athletically with having to shoulder the cost of my own college education created a strong desire to move out and on, so I headed to Madison. For the next three years, I worked two and sometimes three jobs, went to school, and joined a fraternity. As an 18-year-old, my motivations were simple: money, power, and sex. My goal in life was to be the wealthiest man in the world.

Reading this, you may find it humorous as I do, but it was true. Respect and love in my family was earned by accomplishment; if I was rich, then I would be loved and respected. Little did I know at the time what a dead-end road that would lead me down.

An Unexpected Change

Early on in Madison, I met a thirty-year-old man who had made a million dollars in a network marketing business. Half an hour with him convinced me, *If this guy can make a million dollars, I can make ten.* I signed up, jumped in, and took off, and for the next couple of years I focused on building my business. The best way to describe me was as a driven person who used people and loved things.

I continued on this path until I was stopped cold one February day when a woman I had been dating looked at me and said, "I'm pregnant; it's your child and I'm going to have an abortion." *Wow.* Up to this point, I thought I could control everything. I had made Emerson's essay, "Self-Reliance," my personal manifesto, and Henley's poem "Invictus" my creed. Now I had a problem, but for two hundred and fifty dollars and a ride to the clinic my problem would be solved—or so I thought.

The next day, looking in the mirror, I saw the face of a murderer. I could not reconcile what I had done. The seven months following were the longest and loneliest I can ever remember. I was gripped with feelings of anxiety and emptiness. During that time, my personal philosophy of life was put to the test and it was found wanting. I was wrestling with the meaning of life. This wrestling match led me down a dark road and the light did not return until September 12, 1982, almost seven months post the abortion, about the time that baby would have been born.

Business took me to the national convention of the company for which I was a distributor. As was their custom, weekend meetings included a non-denominational church service open to anyone who wished to attend. Since faith in anyone other than myself was an enigma to me, I had no intention of going. My personal battle of fighting the emptiness of my life was being waged in business, where I tried to fill my emptiness with accomplishments and material possessions. In addition, I considered people of faith weak, and wanted nothing to do with them.

This is where providence comes in. My ride home from Kansas City was with three people associated with me in my business. All were people of faith, so they were planning on going to the church service. They told me they were leaving for Minneapolis directly from the service so if I was going to ride with them, I would need to come along. Although I did not appreciate or comprehend the faith they had, I personally liked each of them; each had helped me as I had developed my business. More importantly, they were my ride, so I went along. My intention was to sit in the car and read the Sunday paper while they attended the service.

As providence would have it, it was nearly 100 degrees that day, so to prevent heat stroke, I went into the Kansas City Coliseum where the event was being held and took my newspaper to the top row, as far away from the church service as possible. The sports page that day was filled with all the things the middle of September brings, baseball playoffs, pro and college football . . . a perfect Sunday read.

That is, until I was interrupted by the preacher speaking to those gathered at the other end of the coliseum. One question caught my attention: "Have you ever felt an emptiness in your life?" It was the right question for me that day; my life had lost its meaning and emptiness was the perfect description. I put down the paper and listened as he explained the source of my emptiness. He said, "The emptiness you are feeling is caused by your separation from your creator, God, who created you for a purpose, which is to glorify him. The cause of the separation is *sin.*"

Now, "sin" was not a word I was familiar with whatsoever. However, I was drowning in my empty life, so I continued to listen. The speaker continued, "There is only one way to bridge the gap your sin has created between you and God; your sin must be paid for. But you can't afford the price and God knows it. So, he provided someone who could: his only son, Jesus. He allowed his son to be sacrificed as the penalty and payment for our sins, yours and mine." I was captivated and fully engaged now it was as if he were speaking just to me.

His next question sealed it for me. "Have you ever wished you could start your life over again?" At that moment it was exactly what I wished for, and I would have paid any price to gain a do over, but I had no idea what to do. He told me, "You can start fresh today, with a clean slate as if all your past life had never happened. You only need to do one thing: agree with God that you are a sinner in need of a savior, then believe Jesus paid the penalty for your sins and ask him to save you. Doing so will allow you to reboot your life."

What happened next I barely remember. He said something like, "If anyone here would like to have a do over, come down here now and commit your life to Jesus and you will get a fresh start today." I don't remember running down to the stage, but I must have, since I was the first one there, crying like a baby. That moment I will never forget. I felt a flood of emotion, love, and acceptance I had never experienced before; it was as if I had been freed from a prison cell. My life began again that day. It was the day I experienced the providence of God in a most personal way. The guilt I felt over the abortion fell away, and many other emotional wounds began to heal as well.

My three companions who brought me there did not know what to do with me now that I had joined them in faith and the nine-hour drive home was largely a silent one, but I felt like a new man.

Thanks to Providence

The summer following my reboot, I learned a startling truth about the circumstances of my own birth, which I had always been told was "premature." Unsolicited, three of my mother's closest friends came to me separately and confessed their knowledge that I was an abortion survivor—that my mother, suffering her own emotional pain, had attempted to end her pregnancy with me. It didn't work and, as a result, I am here to write this book today. It is the providence of God that I am alive.

It is also God's providence and grace that enable me to have love and empathy for my mother. I don't know all the circumstances of her life, but I know enough to feel sorry for the emotional abuse she experienced as a child. Although the attempted abortion was a rejection of me, it was also a rejection of her own life and self, born out of the wounds she suffered.

My mom never admitted this to me, but the unvarying story told to me on three separate occasions by three of her closest friends forces me to accept this hard truth. It is a big piece of a puzzle I have struggled to complete in my life, and learning and accepting it has opened the door to emotional healing for me. I never understood why, whenever I was with her, she seemed visibly uncomfortable and agitated, signaling me in her unfiltered way that she would rather be with someone else than with me. I know now that seeing me likely reminded her of the truth, a truth that is painful to confront outside of the forgiveness and grace of God.

What she doesn't understand is that, just as God has forgiven me for my part in an abortion, I have forgiven her for her own abortion attempt. If she would turn to Jesus, she would find He offers her that forgiveness and release too.

I am an abortion survivor because of the providence of God. He had a different plan for me!

My life has not been free from disappointments and struggles, but as a result of my decision, I now have somewhere to go and Someone to ask for help with my daily life. I could not in good conscience write a book such as this without offering the same to you. If you find yourself wrestling with the emptiness of this life, struggling to find meaning in it, and you too would like a reboot, I want you to know that you can have one. You just need to do what I did: admit your sin and separation from God, turn to Jesus and ask him to forgive you, and receive the forgiveness and relationship he offers. You, too, can experience reconciliation with God. It is as simple as that.

Learning to Accept Providence

Over the last several years, God has used adversity in my business life to humble me and free me from self-reliance, and to teach me to be reliant on him. As a Christian, I believe that God is sovereign, and ultimately in control of all things, including my life. I also believe that he created me and because of that he loves me, and he wants the best for me, within the boundaries of his will. So, anything that happens to me must first be filtered through his divine will. As a result, even the bad stuff in life is allowed by him for my good and for His glory.

Learning to recognize and accept providence, accepting what I cannot control and trusting what I cannot see, is a lesson I learned late in life. It was one of those lessons that I was not ready to accept early in my career, but later, when I was ready, the Teacher showed up at just the right time. It was a hard lesson, one I learned the day we decided the right thing was to close the business I had founded and built.

The circumstances we found ourselves in were so unusual that, in the end, I could only explain them as providence. That was the soft pillow I laid my head on each night. We considered sticking it out, but the risk was running our cash to zero and leaving our team with nothing. If we closed, we could pay severance and give them and their families an orderly transition.

So, on a cool, fall weekend in 2016, as the leader, I came to the decision that closing our doors was the right thing to do. Two weeks later, on the day before Thanksgiving, we told the team that, after twenty-three years, we would close at the end of the year. This was the hardest conversation I had ever had. So many things outside of my influence or control contributed to our closure that, even today, as I look back, I can only attribute it to providence.

Are there some things I would have done differently? Absolutely, and I bear that responsibility. But hindsight is 20:20, and, knowing what I know now, even the things I would have done differently would not have helped us; they only would have prolonged the inevitable.

So, I added another lesson learned to my list: I need to accept providence. I am grateful to have learned this lesson, because it has freed me from taking responsibility for a lot of things I cannot control. Doing this leaves me space to focus on what is in my control—and that makes for a better leader, a pro leader.

Leaders are responsible, responsible for so many things: your people, your product, your process, your P&L, and my favorite category: anything else. The problem comes when you take responsibility for things that are truly out of your control; that is a losing effort from the start. As a leader you need to be about winning, so to take on something that is clearly a no-win is a foolish waste of time.

As I've mentioned before, when I sit down and plan my week ahead, I first write down my WIN—What's Important Now. I have learned that what's important now are the things that I can control; those activities that help to fulfill the call and responsibilities of my life. What is not important are the many things that are out of my control; those I leave to providence. I have wasted too much time in my life and my career trying to influence things that are out of my control. Once, I stopped that, life got simpler and better.

The result of understanding and accepting providence is peace. No longer do I need to be about what I call anxious striving. Now I know the reason my striving caused anxiety; it was due to the fact that what I was striving for was out of my control.

A peaceful leader is a relaxed leader, and a good leader. I see this principle embodied on one of my favorite shows, *The Dog Whisperer*, with Caesar Milan. Caesar demonstrates often how calm and assertive leadership is the key to leading dogs: "Your calm keeps them calm," he says. Well, I have found that it's not so different when leading people: my calm keeps them calm—and nothing makes for calm better than knowing what you can control and what you cannot.

My recommendation: come to terms with providence, however you need to do that. But *do* it. It will bring peace and calm to your life and to your leadership, and you will be a better leader because of it.

Principle Application

1. How would you say you have experienced providence?

2. Take a look at your current life situation. What things are outside your control?

3. Where do you need to "let go" or simply loosen your grip?

4. Where/what/whom do you turn to find peace?

15 | The Downside of Consensus

"Consensus is the absence of leadership"
—Margaret Thatcher

> **PRO LEADERSHIP PRINCIPLE:** Consensus is a
> wise servant but a foolish master.

As an entrepreneur in the investment world, I clearly understood that the consensus estimate of a company's earnings was an average—that is, the "mean" of all of the analysts' estimates of the future earnings of that company. The larger the company, the more analysts would cover it; as a result there were more estimates, and the consensus estimate would be trusted by a larger number of investors.

The problem with this estimate was that, while it would often be directionally correct, it was rarely precise, and this caused a lot of consternation in the markets. Think volatility: you have probably read of a company's stock being down, say, five percent in a day, after having released earnings and missing the consensus estimate by a single penny. Ridiculous. In the long-run what does one penny matter? It doesn't, but greed and fear believe it does, and since those are ultimately the two drivers of the stock market, one penny matters, and so does consensus.

Therein lies the problem with consensus. As an investment professional, I learned that to manage to consensus was a sure way to be average, and average is a loser in business—you cannot win that way. But today, so much of our world is seeking consensus, either because they are trying to please everyone, or they are afraid of being wrong and having to suffer for it.

This is why pro leaders understand that consensus is a wise servant but a foolish master. As a result of this understanding, the best leaders don't manage to consensus; they lead to excellence—and excellence is rarely borne of consensus.

Consensus as a Tool, Not a Driver

In thirty plus years of business, I grew to hate consensus, but experience has taught me that, when leading people, it can be a powerful tool. It is, however, a tool requiring time, patience, and skill in the hands of a leader. Like any tool, it may be used for good or for bad.

The principle I learned first as an investment professional, I later came to see as also useful in life and in overall leadership. In leadership terms, allowing consensus to drive your decision is similar to decision-making by committee. Consider for a minute the last committee you were a member of. In the end, what did you accomplish? Excellence, or average?

I have to admit I hate committees (of course I do, I have entrepreneurial DNA!). Well, I do not really hate committees; it is what committees are so often pulled together to produce that I hate—that is, a middle ground, a "good enough," or, "something we can all agree on." Have you ever seen anything that "we can all agree on" that you have been excited about?

That being said, there is a path to a good and beneficial consensus, one that can be a growth catalyst to an organization or a movement. But to achieve it takes patience and time. These days, those are two qualities caught in the torrent of change in a world driven by the "Amazonization" of everything, making them increasingly rare. I love a quote to this effect from one of my heroes, Margaret Thatcher, former prime minister of Great Britain during the time Ronald Reagan was president of the United States. It was Thatcher who said, "Consensus is the absence of leadership"—a wonderful truth.

Why are we so often motivated to achieve consensus? It's likely because, as leaders, to be successful, we need followers to follow us, and most people will not follow (for long, anyway) an idea they don't agree with. So, to be effective, a leader must build a consensus among his or her followers. But remember this key point: **building is different from achieving.** A wise leader will initially seek and measure consensus to gain agreement and momentum—that is smart. But to wait on a decision until you achieve consensus—that is not always smart, and will often result in missed opportunities.

The Oxford Dictionary defines consensus as "general agreement." Agreement is a good thing when the emphasis is on the word "general." Where I experienced difficulty as a leader was when I waited to accomplish *specific* and *absolute* agreement before making a decision. I came to understand why my dad used to say, "A leader makes a decision; sometimes he makes the right decision, and sometimes he makes the wrong decision, but he always makes a decision." If I deferred a decision because I didn't have consensus, that in itself was a decision—and not usually a good one.

Since consensus is the mean, it looks safe. The middle of the road often looks safe, doesn't it? But in business, "safe" is often overcome by courage—someone else's. And then what looked safe, will, in hindsight, look foolish.

The reality is that a pro leader must have advice, and his or her advisors must be willing to speak the truth as they know it, but they need not all agree; the decision is up to the leader. Experience has taught me that rarely is the consensus view the correct view. It may be the safe view, but it is rarely the winning view. Leading by consensus may look like a winner today, but can often end up a loser tomorrow.

So, how can a leader use consensus as a tool in decision-making, rather than as a driver? First of all, it's important to remember the key definition of consensus: *general* agreement. The exercise of developing a strategic vision for your company results in a *general* strategy for accomplishing the mission. This includes the type of business you will be, the people you will need, the product you will sell, the processes you will use, and the revenue and profit you expect to generate. The initial strategic vision should be general, light on tactical detail—details come later, as the vision is accepted and as you influence your team around it. This is where you use your influence to build consensus. That consensus that is the natural outcome of the specific inputs of your individual team members is what makes it work, turning a brake into an accelerator.

Beginning with a strategic vision, and then building consensus—general agreement—around it with your team is vital to its fulfillment. But once the journey has begun, leadership must move forward with the understanding that consensus is a wise servant but a foolish master. It is a necessary tool in decision-making, but it should not be the driver of it. To draw on another analogy, it belongs in the back seat, not the driver's seat!

Where Consensus Bogs Down

Was Thatcher correct, that consensus is the absence of leadership? As leaders, we need to build it (consensus), but also must know that we will never achieve it before it is time to start moving. In fact, as we build an organization, and our team, consensus-building grows more difficult, not less. Why? People.

Each unique individual you add to your team brings his or her own set of experiences and opinions. The more opinions sitting around the table, the more time and patience it will take to achieve consensus. Because of this, remember that achieving absolute consensus is not the goal; building it is, and 85 percent is good enough (See Chapter 17 for a discussion of the 85 percent rule in decision making).

For Ronald Reagan, his rule was 70 percent. His leadership strategy was, "Get me 70 percent of what we desire and that is good enough to go—we can work on getting the remaining 30 percent over time." Like Reagan, pro leaders are consensus builders, but when the time comes for a decision, they don't need 100 percent agreement to make it.

But the building of consensus is only one ingredient of good decision-making. The differing opinions you will hear from your leadership team in an effort to reach a general agreement on a strategy or a tactic are components of a good decision. Failure to consider those opinions often leads to a regret. Be willing to hear them all, consider them all, and you will be better able to make a wise decision.

When I started my asset management company, we were classic consensus thinkers—never wanting to get too far from it for fear of making a big mistake; we wanted to protect the "downside." This sounded good to clients who trusted us to manage some, and in many cases all, of their investments. It also gave us comfort that we would not go too far wrong with any one investment decision.

What we did not appreciate as much was the art of contrary thinking, and how much it plays into good investment and business decision-making. When I first entered the business world, my boss and mentor used to say, "You need to buy your straw hat in the winter time." Later, he recommended a book to me by Humphrey Neill, *The Art of Contrary Thinking: It Pays to Be Contrary*. It is one of the few books I have read multiple times, and I believe it should be on every pro leader's reading list. In it, Neill points out the problem with consensus thinking: it is not contrary. Therefore, the good ideas—the new cutting-edge ideas that will make the biggest impact on your business—will, if you remain a consensus thinker, end up belonging to someone else.

This perspective actually gave me an aversion to consensus for awhile. But, as my business career continued and my responsibilities grew, I had to re-think my attitude toward it, and I eventually came to a more moderate understanding. Although I still agreed that leading by it will do more harm than good, I also recognized it is a useful tool in decision-making, and that I would be unwise to ignore it or fail to consult it.

A Moderate Approach to Consensus

How much consensus needs to be built? Is it 70 percent, as Reagan said, or the 85 percent I aim for? The answer is . . . it depends! Every situation is different. That's where each leader's experience, judgment, and wisdom come into play.

One of my favorite leadership quotes is from Dwight D. Eisenhower, then the Supreme Allied Commander in Europe in World War II. He said, "I like to make mistakes very slowly." He is known as one of history's greatest leaders, and many historians credit him with the Allied victory in Europe, and then, as president, with keeping the peace in the beginnings of the Cold War. He was recognized as a consensus builder, using it as a key step in his decision-making process.

As Eisenhower led the planning for the Allied invasion of Europe in WWII, it was a model of consensus-building. The number and diversity of people involved, the multiple constituencies he had to consider, and the egos he had to manage were vast—and he succeeded in large part due to his ability to build consensus. However, as important as it was, he did not allow consensus to make the decision for him, it only *informed his decision.*

Stephen Ambrose in his extensive biography, *Eisenhower— Soldier President*, details the consensus Eisenhower built prior to the D-Day invasion. He wrote about how the decision to invade on June 6th, 1944 was Eisenhower's alone; in fact, the decision went against the consensus opinions of his general staff. However, the decision proved to be the right one, while hindsight proved the consensus had been wrong.

In this situation, Eisenhower built general consensus and although there remained disagreement over his decision, once he made it, even those who had a different opinion were able to stand behind and support it. The power of Eisenhower's personality, his EQ, and his demonstrated respect for the opinions of his team resulted in their full support of his decision. He proved the principle that achieving *absolute* consensus, which leads to mediocrity, is entirely different than building *general* consensus, which is what all strong leaders are charged to do.

As a leader, if you make it your goal to achieve absolute consensus, you will never get there; you simply will have wasted valuable time and resources trying to accomplish something that simply cannot be done. On the other hand, if you build consensus before you start executing on the plan, you will have gained buy-in from your team—another key to the success of the mission.

Remember, consensus building is a relational skill, because you are building agreement of people on your team or your organization. As you understand the role of each one of your team members and encourage them to share their opinions from their area of strength, as you draw them out, listen to and respond to their opinions, you gain a valuable resource in decision-making.

Pro leaders should be comfortable with listening to—and holding in tension—differing opinions, because they know good decisions require them. When coaching, I like to encourage teams by saying, "If we all agree, we are probably wrong, and if we all agree, we probably are not all necessary." Differing opinions are not problems to be solved, rather, they are a tension to be managed. Like most tensions, they are managed through relationships with your team, as a whole and one-on-one. It is an exercise of EQ over IQ, soft skills over hard skills. Any relationship-building takes time and patience, and a pro leader will allow both.

Just as leadership is a people business, building consensus is too. A pro leader builds consensus and people at the same time. It is accomplished best nose to nose, one individual at a time. Do that and you can reach consensus in any group.

We have returned to where we started. As a leader, it is up to you to cast the vision, and then lead your team toward the vision by building relationships with them and giving them ownership of it through building consensus. This process acknowledges and values their opinions on how the mission and vision will be accomplished.

In the end, the wisdom of Thatcher's leadership has been validated by history, and I believe what she said about consensus is correct. Without leadership, consensus takes over. When that happens, a mission rarely succeeds, because consensus is a wise servant but a foolish master. To lead with impact, a pro leader will need to understand this principle. In addition, he or she will need to communicate it well to all her constituencies, and this is the subject of the next chapter as you grow and lead with impact.

Principle Application

1. How do others' views and opinions influence your leadership?

2. How has consensus building helped or hindered your leadership?

3. How much consensus is enough for you to make a decision?

4. What do you see as the role of consensus in your decision making? Has that changed since reading this chapter?

16 | Communicate[3]

"What we've got here is failure to communicate."
—The Captain's speech, *Cool Hand Luke* (1967)

> **PRO LEADERSHIP PRINCIPLE:** When we fail to communicate, we fail to communicate.

Twenty years ago, I sat in a Stephen Covey workshop and drafted my personal mission statement. This exercise consisted defining all of the "roles of play" in my life that could benefit from a mission statement for each one. When I finished, I had condensed my numerous roles to four: husband, father, leader, and friend. Each clarifying statement helped to clearly define my role in that relationship. Though it might sound tedious to some, I found it incredibly impactful.

In my role as a leader, the clarifying statement was, in part: *I will be professional, and I will promote and develop excellence in an encouraging, win-win environment in all four areas of my responsibility: 1) Setting Standards, 2) Setting Expectations, 3) Measuring Results and Holding Accountable, and 4) Communicating and Delivering Rewards and Consequences.*

I have remained in a leader role, in one way or another, since the day I identified it at the workshop. Today the only change is its clarifying statement. Experience has driven and demanded each revision, but its current version has essentially remained unchanged for the past decade. Two major realizations led to my current purpose statement: one, my role as a leader will always be relational, and two, success in my role is completely dependent on clear communication. If I fail in either of these two areas, I will fail in my role as a leader, because mastering communication is required to lead with impact.

One of the many tensions I must manage in my personality is a tendency to be a "lone ranger," often expressed as an attitude of, "If it is to be, it is up to me." This is a perfectionist trait, one I was once proud of, but now I see it differently. Experience has tamed my perfectionist ways. In the past, I rarely believed anyone could do anything as well as I could, so I ended up doing everything—or trying to do everything—myself, which is a common tendency of an entrepreneur. My coach Bill Berman helped me with this when he taught me the 85 percent principle (which is the subject of the next chapter). **The 85 percent rule is this: if someone on my team is able to do a task 85 percent as well as I can, I should probably not be doing it.** Rather, as the leader, I should prioritize and do things only I can do. I share this personal example because of the impact it has on communication. Acting as a "lone-ranger" harms one's ability to lead in two ways: it damages relationships and blocks communication, resulting in frustration and, often, the stagnation of the mission.

Prioritizing Relationships through Communication

Relationships are damaged often for one simple reason: the application of perfectionism means no one's work, including your own, is accepted as good enough. Through the lens of perfectionism, you become that priggish editor, never satisfied, always editing the work, and in the end, straining away the personality of the one who originated the work.

I once listened to an interview of author Stephen King; it was fascinating! King said something I have never forgotten and consider a great leadership lesson. He said, "To write is human, to edit is divine," and then went on to describe what separated good editors from great ones (and of course, he considered his editor one of the greats). "A great editor will not change the writer, or what has been written, but will edit in such a way that she brings out the best of the author. On the other hand, the good editor, though correct in the application of the English language—probably an honors student in Advanced Placement, makes so many edits that the personality of the author is eliminated—and that destroys the work. A great editor enhances the author's ability to communicate."

In my early years of leadership, I was like that "good editor," taking everyone's work and making such a complete "re-write" that they could no longer recognize anything they had created. Do this to people long enough, and they will not be willing to put their heart into their work, because, they know you are just going to "break it" in the end. This leads to poor work, further frustrating a perfectionist leader. I know; I have been on both sides and have experienced relationships being damaged, leadership being hindered, and communication breaking down.

This is how I learned this particular pro leadership principle: **when we fail to communicate, we fail to communicate.**

Setting Standards and Expectations

I want to continue on through my clarifying statement for my role as a leader: *setting standards and setting expectations.* Unless we communicate clearly, we will find it difficult to succeed in setting standards and expectations. Here is yet another lesson I learned the hard way. I had developed the initial grand vision for my firm, formulated the strategy, and identified the tactics I thought best to win. Then, I went to work and expected everyone else to follow me and just do it. The problem was, I had failed not only to build consensus, but also to clearly communicate the vision and the strategy, leaving most of my team's understanding of it up to their own imaginations. What a fool I was! Imagine a drum major enthusiastically marching at the head of the band, but no one is following. That was me. Principle applied; lesson learned.

Today, as head coach of my own leadership consulting firm, I coach clients to lead differently than I did. I like to tell them, "It is cheaper for you to learn from my mistakes than it is to learn by making them yourself." Once you have formulated the vision, involve your team in developing the strategy and the tactics. Slow down, build consensus, gain buy-in, and focus on the vision and the mission, again and again and again. Business leader Adena Friedman put it well, "Ideas are only as good as your ability to communicate them." This is a superb application of Communication^3 = Communicate, Communicate, Communicate, and the pro leadership principle: When we fail to communicate, we fail to communicate.

I once interviewed a retired CEO of a Fortune 50 company. I asked him, "What is the biggest leadership challenge you have faced?" Without a moment's hesitation, he smiled and said, "leading myself." Whether you are willing to admit it or not, this is every leader's biggest challenge. Nowhere does self-leadership become more important than in the application of this principle of communication; it is a continuous process requiring consistent self-discipline. But, be encouraged: winning the communication battle is a strategy with three steps any leader can take: simply **plan, prepare, and practice**. With desire, will, time, and patience, every pro leader has within them the ability to master communication and doing so, will give your leadership impact.

I learned this from studying Winston Churchill, one of my heroes, who may be the greatest communicator who ever lived in the twentieth century, if not all of history. His ability to communicate turbo-charged his leadership and helped him to influence millions, which mobilized a movement to confront the evils of Hitler and then, communism. Reading his many works, one quickly realizes that he was able to say more in one sentence than most can say in a full page. Thanks to technology, many of his masterful speeches are now available online for us all to learn from. I always think of Churchill when I plan, prepare, and practice my own communication. Here's how I do it:

Plan. All pro leadership begins with planning. And, pro leaders plan with the end in mind. What is the best outcome of your communication? What impression do you want to make and what action do you desire to influence? What about timing: When is the best time to communicate so your message will have maximum impact? Be strategic about your method of communication—in this digital age, we have never before had so many communication formats, and it has never before been more critical to communicate in the "right" way. If you miss the mark here, your powerful message may be lost in translation in your method of communicating was not appropriate.

Prepare. Churchill once said, "I spend a good portion of my free time preparing my extemporaneous remarks." Master communicators even prepare what, to others, appears unprepared. This looks different for everyone. For some, it may mean memorizing key phrases or points. For others, it means taking notes. In some situations, it may mean researching statistics, facts, or figures, so your message has a foundation of truth and is backed by numbers. For most, planning consists of big ideas (think whiteboard), while preparing consists of actually writing your message or portions of your message out. John Wooden, who, as coach of the UCLA Bruins won ten national championships, said, "When opportunity comes, it is too late to prepare." This is also true in communication and why preparation is so vital to its success.

Practice. Once planned and prepared, you are ready to act on the plan. The more you practice the better you will play, and this is true in every discipline in both life, sports, and business. Electronics have made practicing communication incredibly simple to do. I like to call my cell phone and deliver my message, then listen to it to see how it sounds. Once it's over, I ask myself how I would feel if I heard this message as an employee or team member. I give it standing up; I give it sitting down. I sit in front of my computer and record myself, noticing my expressions and my timing. Practice makes perfect? Maybe, maybe not, but practice *does* help you be more relaxed, which will lead to you being yourself, and this is a major key to impactful communication.

How Leaders Communicate

Let's look back at the four responsibilities I identified in my clarifying statement regarding the role of a leader, and see how these responsibilities might benefit from planning, preparing, and practice in communication. Those responsibilities are: *1) Setting Standards 2) Setting Expectations. 3) Measuring Results and Holding Accountable 4) Communicating and Delivering Rewards and Consequences.*

A leader's communication can have maximum positive impact through **setting standards**, which is an absolute top-down responsibility. It starts with the leader and it is a cultural activity; that is, it sets the tone for the entire organization. I will never forget listening to Bill George speak about this when he was CEO of Medtronic, one of the world's leading medical device companies. At the time he was also teaching a seminar on Ethics at the Harvard Business School.

On this particular day, he was speaking about setting standards for the company he led. "At Medtronic," he said, "we do not have the luxury of being 99 percent accurate in our manufacturing process, because if we get one percent wrong, people die. Therefore, we seek excellence and for us, that number is 100 percent." I have heard it confirmed from people who worked in the industry and at Medtronic that this was the message George preached daily. "If we aren't perfect, people will die, and we can't live with that." The message was communicated face to face, in an absolutely riveting speech he had clearly prepared to have maximum impact—which it did.

I would not be doing justice to communication without mentioning another master communicator, Ronald Reagan, perhaps the most effective communicator I have experienced in my lifetime. His philosophy was simple, 1) tell them what you are going to tell them, 2) tell them, 3) tell them what you told them. Then tomorrow and the next day, repeat the message.

Bottom line: when building culture and setting standards, face to face is the place to start. Consistency and follow through reinforce it. Any other methods will be icing on the cake to make sure your initial message sets a tone and culture others can identify with and replicate.

Setting expectations can be both a strategic and a tactical endeavor, and the manner of communicating may be different, depending upon which one it is; however the planning is the same for both. When a leader is simply establishing the desired outcome of a specific tactical operation, it may not be necessary for face-to-face communication. In addition, the speed of business may not allow time for it, in which case a well-crafted email written in a clear, positive tone may be appropriate. However, with ready access to video conferencing, face-to-face communication can happen anytime, so I coach whenever possible to start every communication face to face and use all other methods for reinforcement and follow-up of the message.

Communicating when *measuring results and holding people accountable* is often left to dashboards, financial statements, and sales spreadsheets. I have often had leaders tell me, "I let the numbers do my talking for me." I don't recommend pro leaders operate this way. Rather, if the results are strong, look at this as an opportunity to promote, recognize, and encourage your team. On the other hand, if the results have not met your expectations, to quote Churchill, "Never waste a good crisis." Understand that misses are a part of the business of life, and are opportunities to communicate the same things you communicated in the win: promote, recognize, and encourage:

- *Promote* the plan, and any course corrections needed to accomplish the mission.
- *Recognize* what you did right, what you would do differently, and what you are going to change.
- *Encourage* by separating the people from the outcome and making yourself available to coach or for support, if needed.

Let this attitude guide your application of **communicating and delivering rewards and consequences**. Leadership and life are not always problem-free, so leaders have to plan to communicate not only the good, but the bad—and sometimes the ugly—truth. Pro leaders don't fear the truth because they know the truth brings freedom. If you are going to be free to win, you will also be free to lose, and a leader needs to be able to communicate positively no matter how difficult the message. This is yet another reason why good communication is so important. The good messages are easy, and it doesn't take a pro leader to communicate them well. But the tough messages demand a pro—one who can bring truth with grace to a difficult situation and finish with the team buoyed and ready to get back to work.

One more thought: oftentimes, our communication comes through much more than our words. We convey a great deal through the tone of our voice and our body language. Be sensitive to how you may be communicating in these ways; it is much more important than you may realize!

This is good, simple advice that pro leaders will all apply when they understand this Pro Leadership Principle: When we fail to communicate, we fail to communicate.

--- **Principle Application** ---

1. Recall a time when you communicated well and it paid off. What made that communication effective?

2. Next, recall a time you wish you had communicated better. What would have made it better?

3. How would you grade your communication skills? Why?

4. What would strengthen your communication skills?

17 | Decision-Making at the Speed of Business

"Indecision and delays are the parents of failure."
—George Canning

> **PRO LEADERSHIP PRINCIPLE:** Indecision in not an option for a leader.

France Avenue is the main street of Edina, Minnesota, which was, for a time, the headquarters of my company. While France Avenue stretched over two hundred blocks from north to south through Minneapolis and its surrounding suburbs, thirty-eight of those blocks ran through Edina, and sixteen through the heart of the commercial district—Class A retail and office space. City planners, bowing to pressure from retailers, had set the traffic lights so that if one drove the speed limit, one was guaranteed to stop at a majority of the lights. The merchants and the city reasoned that, if you must stop, you might shop. It didn't happen; instead, it only angered drivers and residents.

The painful traffic management experiment lasted three years, until one woman ran for mayor. Her campaign platform had only one plank; synchronize the stoplights on France Avenue. She lost, but had such strong support for her plank all the other candidates were forced to adopt it. As a result, one week following the election, the lights were synchronized so that if you drove the speed limit you could go from one end to the other without stopping.

It was during this time we were wrestling with some business decisions which required buy-in from one of our senior leaders. He had been tasked with doing the research and making a final recommendation but was caught by indecision. Like all important business decisions, time was of the essence. I wrestled with simply making the decision for him but had learned the demoralizing effect this tactic can have on another leader, especially if they are doing good work. However, his indecision was beginning to cause frustration among our senior leadership team. The situation needed leadership.

My favorite leadership tactic is leadership by walking around. The beauty of a small company was the ability for me to see every one of my associates every day I was in the office. Learning this practice from my mentor, I took the first hour of every business day and walked around and "checked in" with all of my associates. For some, I would do nothing more than smile and ask, "How are you?" Or, thank them for some work they had done or a project they had contributed to. But, for others, who may have been struggling with some life or work issue, I used it as an opportunity to encourage or offer to help.

These were my favorite hours of my days; I loved the connection it created between my associates and me. So, as one of my leaders struggled with indecision, leadership by walking around provided me with a natural opportunity to help him through his decision road block.

When I came to his office, I stepped in, sat down, and said, "I know you have been pouring yourself into this research;

how far are you from making a recommendation?" He quickly took me through his work, highlighting the pros and cons. He had clearly done excellent work. He hadn't missed any of the majors, but he was hung up on a few minors, and analysis paralysis was preventing a recommendation.

"Let's take a walk," I said. He followed me out the door and out to the corner of France Avenue and 78th Street. We took the crosswalk and stopped on the median. Looking north, I asked, "How many traffic lights do you see?"

He replied, "I cannot see them all, but I know there are sixteen."

Then I asked him, "If you were driving, how many of the lights would need to be green in order for you to go?"

"Just the one in front of me," he replied.

Now it was my turn to lead. "Maybe the recommendation you are wrestling with is the same; you are waiting for all the lights to be green and it will never happen. You may simply need the next one to be green so you can get started." He smiled and laughed, thanked me and we walked back into the office.

Two hours later, at a gathering of the senior leadership team, he made his recommendation. He had learned a valuable lesson in leadership: if you wait for all the lights to be green, you will rarely go anywhere. He learned the pro leadership principle: *Indecision is not an option.*

Leaders (Must) Make Decisions

Leaders make decisions. Sometimes they are right and sometimes they are wrong, but they always make a decision. Decision-making is their primary responsibility. Pro leaders know this. Not only are leaders required to make decisions, but those decisions must be made at the "speed of business," and with the world today moving faster and faster, the risks to good decision-making are greater than they have ever been. But those risks will only continue to grow as the speed of business grows. Today we are in the middle of an information revolution. Thanks to the internet, information has become ubiquitous, and intelligence is swiftly being commoditized. The drive to artificial intelligence will require leaders to be more than smart; to win they will need to be wise. Those who possess wisdom will gain an advantage over those who don't. Those who rely on "brains" alone will not be able to keep up. Why? Because we were not designed to move as fast as the world is now moving.

Consider this example. At the company I helped to build, analysts covered all of the sectors and industries of the global economy. Each analyst had a unique personality, but one common denominator united them: they were brilliant. An analyst is to the investment business what a process engineer is to a manufacturing company. I lovingly referred to them all as "Sheldon," from the popular TV show *Big Bang Theory.*

For analysts to succeed, they must have access to and be able to process large amounts of information. It requires an intellectual curiosity to drive them deeper and deeper into their research, but they also need to know when to say, "Enough," and make a recommendation.

But, when information is unlimited, the boundaries of research expand, making the decision to say, "Enough," more difficult. In my final year as leader of our company, the average senior analyst received over one million research emails. They were buried in information, and it directly affected their decision-making ability. There was too much information. Too much information added a new level of stress to an already stressful business.

We have reached the edge of the envelope; added intelligence no longer adds value, it simply drains energy—the energy we need to succeed. To lead with impact, a leader must have energy, and energy does not come from information.

Seek Wisdom

You see, the pursuit of knowledge will drain you. But wisdom? That's another story. Seek *wisdom* and you will be energized. That is why at Andrew Wyatt Leadership, when asked what we do, we say, "We transform *smart* leaders into *wise* leaders." Intelligence is assumed, but nothing succeeds like wisdom.

How is a wise decision made? How do you make it at the speed of business? The answers are simple, but not easy, unless you have done the work in the first section of this book (excavation before elevation). That's because wise decisions begin with you, the leader. Wisdom is an inside-out character trait. All inside-out decisions require two ingredients: knowing yourself and knowing your why. Together these two principles drive decision-making; they are the key to wise decisions.

Do you know of Wilber Ross, the billionaire American industrialist and Secretary of Commerce in the Trump Administration? He is the one who was asked, "What is the secret to your success?" and he responded, "Wise decisions."

The interviewer immediately shot-back, "How did you learn to make wise decisions?"

With his famous classic brevity, he responded, "Unwise decisions."

For Ross and for any pro leader, the difference between a wise and an unwise decision is, more often than not, knowing yourself and knowing your why. In fact, it would be a wise idea to review Chapters 3 and 4 of this book, and to consider their role in how you make decisions. Regardless, let's look at each and how they contribute to wise decision-making.

Business Brilliant by Lewis Schiff is a wonderful book; I ask all of my prospective coaching clients to read it before we begin a relationship. In it, Schiff masterfully presents a number of business icons, how they made it, what drove them, and how they made decisions. Unique from many business biographies, it shows the out-of-the-box thinking and decision-making that led to the success of these people.

Yes, all were immensely competent, and all had entrepreneurial DNA, but they all had one other unique characteristic that contributed greatly to their success: **each was a rugged individualist.** They each knew themselves; they knew who they were and who they were not. Why does that matter? Because it kept them from doing things that were not natural to them. It allowed them to say no to anything that did not match their essence.

Saying no is a key to saying yes. It is an application of the 80:20 principle. It applies here too. Our time is limited; to have impact, we must focus on our highest and best priority. This requires we say no to the majority of opportunities that present themselves to us—otherwise we will not have time and space to say yes to the 20 percent of activities which create 80 percent of our impact.

As I have interviewed business leaders, I like to ask at what point they began to experience success and, as a follow-up, what factor had the greatest impact on their success. Although their specific situations and answers have been different, a common thread is found in all. Those leaders who have experienced a significant loss or a set-back, and have persevered and recovered, will tell me the tide turned for them when they finally realized who they were and who they were not and began to make decisions on that basis. Warren Buffett is a perfect example of his own investment maxim: *Don't invest in businesses you don't understand.* Having followed Buffett over my whole career, I have heard him say often when asked why he chose not to invest, "That's just not me." Knowing yourself is a key to saying no and knowing that helps you know when to say yes. That's good wisdom.

Knowing your why has the same effect on decision-making: if you know your why, you know why not. When a leader knows her why, she will not be distracted by anything that does not fit, and if she is, it won't take long for the truth to be revealed that this is not a fit. For this reason, Simon Sinek's book, *Start with Why*, is the second book I ask all prospective coaching clients to read before our first session, not only to help them to discover their own why, but because I know the effect discovering one's why has on wise decision-making.

Applying Wisdom to Our Decision-Making

In life and in business, time is of the essence. Nowhere is that more true than in decision-making. John Maxwell is famous for responding to a question about how he manages time by saying, "I don't. We cannot manage time, we can only manage ourselves and our priorities." Wise decisions are ones made on time, at the speed of business. Knowing yourself is vital to maximizing one's ability to be "on time" in decision-making.

Let me give you a personal example. In Chapter 3, "Know Yourself," we looked at a self-knowledge tool, the Enneagram. I related that I test as an Eight (The Leader) and, in times of strength, I go to a Two (The Helper). However, in times of weakness, I go to Five (The Investigator). When I have a decision to make, and I find myself stuck in indecision, I have learned it is often because there is some imbalance in my life and I have moved to Five; I have become overly analytical, and generally I am instinctively a gut-level decision-maker. When I think too long, I stall out. So, when I recognize that trait being played out, I realize balance needs to be restored to my life. When I take the actions necessary to restore balance, I return to my strength and decisions become clear, and I act in a helpful way.

The template for wise decision-making is: know yourself, know your why, have a 80:20 no to yes ratio, and, finally apply the 85 percent rule. All that being said, no human has ever had complete knowledge when making a decision, and no one ever will, so don't expect to. All the lights will never be green, and if you wait, you will never go anywhere.

Two versions of the 85 percent rule occupy my leadership toolbox. The first application is that a leader should not be executing any task which someone else in the organization could do 85 percent as well. A leader's highest and best use of time is to do only those tasks only you can do. But the second derivative of the 85 percent rule is that decisions need to be made with 85 percent of the information. Even today, with ubiquitous information, 85 percent of what we need to know to make a wise decision is readily available to us. The key of course is to determine the information that matters most.

That is where wisdom comes in. Remember, wisdom = information + experience + judgment. Colin Powell, former

Chairman of the Joint Chiefs in the Reagan Administration and Secretary of State in the Bush administration, was famous for his decision-making ability. Powell said his advantage was the ability to make decisions with only 65 percent of the information; he could because he understood the 65 percent that mattered most.

Becoming comfortable with 85 percent decision-making takes practice, but, as a leader, your impact will grow the more often you are able to do it. If you have accurate information, if you have had experience and have learned from it, you will develop judgment, which makes the probability of a wise decision higher. Combine that with knowing yourself, and knowing how you instinctively make decisions, and the stress of making a decision will be reduced.

The Decisions after the Decision

Finally, no discussion of decision-making would be complete without dealing with the post-decision period. It is said Eisenhower never doubted a decision until after he made it; he synthesized information, asked the right questions, listened to his advisors, and then made the decision. It wasn't until after the decision was made that he would wrestle with it being right or not.

History tells us more of Eisenhower's decisions were right than wrong, but his method teaches a valuable leadership lesson. Indecision is not an option for a pro-leader, but good decision-making requires the leader to be intellectually ruthless in post-decision analysis. "I like to make mistakes very slowly, and to correct them quickly," is another Eisenhower saying. Once a decision is made and acted upon, it is incumbent upon the leader to analyze the results and to make any necessary course corrections along the way. The point? Leadership doesn't end with making the decision. Pro leaders measure the results and move quickly to make needed course corrections.

We will end here where we started. A leader's role is to make decisions. Sometimes they are right and sometimes they are wrong, but they always make a decision because indecision is not an option. Pro leaders always keep their options open—and that is the topic of that next chapter.

Principle Application

1. What do you like about decision making?

2. What is your biggest challenge to making a decision?

3. What do you tend to be afraid of?

4. What is the worst business decision you have ever made? How did it help you grow in leadership?

5. What is the best business decision you have ever made? What made it good?

18 | Leave Yourself Options

"Preserve the President's options. He may need them."
—Donald Rumsfeld

PRO LEADERSHIP PRINCIPLE: Leaders leave themselves options.

Recently, I had the chance to spend some time with a lifelong friend (of 50 years, to be exact!). It had been several years since we had been together, as he worked on the other side of the world, but thanks to Zoom, we reconnected, and it felt just like old times.

That's because our relationship is the kind of friendship where, even if you haven't spoken for months or even years, when you reconnect, the conversation picks right up where it left off. In this case, we were talking about our life experiences. He asked me how I would sum up what I had learned in three decades in the investment world. My answer surprised even myself by the first thing that came out of my mouth: "All markets are driven by greed and fear, cash is king, and debt limits options." It was as simple as that—three decades of experience boiled down to one sentence. If I was giving a lecture, this sentence would be my central idea—not the part about investor sentiment, but rather the part about limiting options.

That's because, unless you are leading an investment firm, as I did, your investment results should have little or no influence on your ability to lead with impact. However, the same cannot be said for cash and debt. Too much of one and not enough of the other has wrecked more promising businesses than we can count, and the anchor that debt can become if wise decisions are not made, will make leading with impact very difficult. This is a lesson I had to learn the hard way. (But, as I often tell my coaching clients: it's cheaper to learn from *my* mistakes than to make them yourself!)

Poor Decisions Make Good Teachers

How did I learn to make good decisions? Poor decisions. I've made plenty, but without them, I don't believe I would have ever written this book or invested my life in leadership development. After thirty-three years in the investment management business, I am an investment professional and know more about money, the capital markets, and investment than 98 percent of the people I meet. I still get the occasional call from someone I either worked with, competed with, or served during my career who will ask, "What do you make of this market?" (Usually they mean the stock market, but not always.)

My answer is the same for everyone: "I don't know. I am not close enough anymore to speak with confidence." Most of the time, they sound disappointed, because they wanted me to give them some comfort, or maybe a tip or two. I don't give investment tips, except one, and it's related to what I just said above about cash and debt. My one tip is this: "Diversify and keep some powder dry." What I mean is, "dry powder"—i.e., cash—leaves you *options*. After all, you just never know what tomorrow will bring.

The company I helped to build was thirteen years old when we hit a barrier to our growth—in our industry we were no longer small, but we weren't large enough to compete at the level we desired. My vision was to transform the company, so we could continue to grow and compete nationally and, ultimately, globally. To fulfill our vision we would need people— highly specialized, experienced professionals, and that would take money.

The institutional asset management business is a funny one. Your product is your investment performance, but few prospective clients will believe a new investment team until they have a three-year track record. As a result, building a competitive product means you have to fund "production" for three years before you can expect the revenue to turn on—and only then if your numbers are better than both the market and your competitors.

Even understanding this truth, we liked our odds, and we had assembled a world-class team led by a proven world-class investor. Our plan was to fund our losses for a few years until the new team's track record was established and we could attract the types of clients we desired. Simple plan. We chose to fund the plan with debt instead of equity so as not to dilute our own ownership.

At the time, and under the circumstances, it was a prudent decision. It was 2006 and all was well; everything we did was moving up and to the right. You know what happened next: 2008 and 2009. Thankfully, we came through the Great Recession well, our strong investment results landing us on the radar screens of some of the world's largest investors. This resulted in strong business growth and us beating our plan.

Nevertheless, the debt we were carrying on our balance sheet made me uncomfortable. We had dodged a bullet in 2008-2009 but the experience had opened my eyes to the possibility that things might not work out as I had planned. That was the frame of mind that led us to form a strategic partnership with a new financial partner. Their part was to take the majority of the debt and give us the distribution platform we lacked. It seemed a wise decision. Until it wasn't.

Two things we could neither anticipate nor control created a perfect storm, leading to the debt becoming a hindrance rather than a help. These situations forced our decisions, limited our ability to fulfill both our mission and vision, and ultimately caused the demise of the company. The silver lining in the big, gray cloud of this experience was in the lessons I learned along the way, and one big one in particular: **Debt limits options, and cash is king.**

The "perfect storm" was the result of the zero-interest rate policy of the U.S. Federal Reserve combined with quantitative easing, which caused the virtual elimination of volatility in the stock market over a three-year period of time. Why? With interest rates at zero, investors were forced into stocks to find returns. The only rational way to invest the great sums of money coming into the stock market and to do it quickly was to buy the index. This one-way investment caused the market to rise steadily while dramatically reducing its historic volatility. However, volatility was the life-blood of our investment strategy. When it disappeared, so did our ability to outperform. Capitalism is a two-way street. The investors who hired us because of out-performance fired us for under-performance. It wasn't personal; it was business.

Applying Lessons Learned

You just read the experience; now let's consider the lessons learned and apply them to our leadership paradigm, so you can be better equipped to lead with impact.

In the end, the lessons I learned then now enable me to inspire and equip leaders by allowing them to benefit from my decisions and my experience, both good and bad. My experience with debt and how it affects one's ability to lead with impact has taught me several lessons:

1. Don't forget this: no one knows the future.
2. Understand what you control and what you don't.
3. Be wise, not fearful or proud.
4. Always match debts with assets.
5. Human capital is not an asset to match with debt.
6. Cash is king.

Reflection and application are the key to a lesson, good or bad, having a positive effect on your ability to lead with impact. So, let's look at each lesson above, answering three questions:

1. What does it say?
2. What does it mean?
3. How will it help you lead with impact?

Don't forget this; no one knows the future. Leaders are required to be visionaries, to think strategically, to know where the puck is going. Our role is planning and leading our team toward the fulfillment of a mission and vision. Yet, no one knows what tomorrow will bring. As Eisenhower said of planning, "All planning is useless once the first bullet is fired." This means a leader holds her plans, strategic or tactical, with a loose grip, always leaving options and room to maneuver. As it applies to the final proformas you develop for your mission and vision, this means as a leader you look at all scenarios with regard to how you are going to finance your mission; you leave yourself options so any one decision won't derail your mission. Leaders who have options can have impact.

Understand what you control and what you don't. A common management maxim is not to spend energy on things you cannot either control or affect. As a leader, you control fewer things than you know, so your energy is better spent on the things you do control and can influence. However, understanding what you *don't* control and the effect it may have on your mission is critical to making wise decisions. A leader whose focus is only on what she controls may end up missing the very thing that will derail the greater mission. For example, a farmer cannot control the weather, but it is a major determinant of success. As a result, a wise farmer considers weather when making each year's farming decisions. For me, I would have been wise to consider the effect monetary policy (not in my control) would have on our ability to manage debt. When you understand what you don't control and how it may affect your leadership, you will be able to develop options and options are vital to leading with impact.

Be wise, not fearful or proud. I love what Mae West said: "Too much of a good thing is wonderful." But it's not true of debt. Leverage can be a good thing, but too much of it can harm you. Used wisely, credit and leverage can greatly benefit your mission and vision. The problem comes when debt is not kept in its proper place. I have never heard a leader regret the fact he or she did not have debt. There are good reasons to stay away from debt, but there are just as many reasons to use it. The way to make a wise decision on whether or not to use it is to take the emotion out of it; don't be either fearful or proud. Rather, respect it; it is a two-edged sword—a good but dangerous tool. As a leader, the appropriate amount of leverage can turbo-charge your growth, helping you to have greater impact; but don't forget: it's a sword that cuts both ways.

Always match debts with assets. Asset liability matching is a wise strategy. Just as it happens personally when you get a mortgage on a home (the house is collateral for the loan), wise leaders do the same when they use leverage as a tool to grow their business. Before committing, answer this question: what asset do we have that could pay this back, if our plan doesn't play out as we expect? A leader who can answer these questions will have options.

Human capital is not an asset to match with debt. A pro leader understands his assets go up and down the elevator every day. Without people, no business can succeed. However, this is one asset that is best not to leverage. Why? Life happens, people change, and people leave—and if your mission is dependent on the performance specific people, and that performance determines your ability to handle debt, you are playing with fire.

Remember my experience? I decided to build a team and used debt to fund this building process, but then circumstances changed, and my team was unable to perform in a manner needed to handle the debt efficiently. This led to my leadership hand being forced and required me to make decisions that I never would have made had I been wiser in my use of capital.

Cash is king. One of the strongest tools to help a leader have impact is a strong and flexible balance sheet. When you have this, you have options; you can be opportunistic and take advantage of situations as they present themselves. I learned this lesson when Lou Gerstner was CEO of IBM. Gerstner had been hired to turn around the struggling company. I recommend you read the book *Elephants Can Dance*; it is Gerstner's own story of the successful turnaround and transformation of an iconic brand and company.

The turnaround resulted in IBM having a strong and flexible balance sheet, which allowed them to be opportunistic. The specific case I remember is their decision to purchase Lotus. When Gerstner announced the deal, it was, at the time, one of the largest software deals ever completed. At the press conference, he described the opportunity the deal presented and its timing.

When he was then asked how they intended to fund the deal, I will never forget Gerstner's response. He deferred the question to his CFO, who very casually responded, "We haven't reached that decision yet, and since we have such a strong balance sheet, we have the option to do it in a way that is best for the business and our shareholders. We will get back to you when we have decided." The truth is, they could have easily done the deal with cash, but they didn't have to; if debt was a better decision, they could have gone that way. The market was not going to tell them what they had to do. That is the power of cash; it is an asset that gives a leader options and options help a leader to have impact.

When Rumsfeld penned the lesson quoted at the beginning of this chapter, he summed up a critical pro leadership principle: **Leaders leave themselves options.** He understood that to lead with impact one needs options.

Applying the lessons of this chapter will give *you* options. It will add margin to your life and to your leadership. Margin is another key to impactful leadership, and that is the subject of our next chapter. So read on, pro leader, and learn how "margin is magic."

Principle Application

1. When have you experienced a situation where you felt you were out of options?

   • How did you feel?

   • How did that affect your leadership?

   • How did that affect your decisions?

2. When have you experienced a time when you had many options?

   • How did you feel?

   • How did that affect your leadership?

   • How did that affect your decisions?

3. What area of your life would benefit from options?

   • How can you add them?

19 | Margin Is Magic

"I love a broad margin to my life."
—Henry David Thoreau

> **PRO LEADERSHIP PRINCIPLE:** Margin makes leadership effective.

I was sitting in the office of the Director of the Sleep Center at the Mayo Clinic in Rochester, Minnesota. I was sent there as a result of an executive physical my board of directors had ordered me to take. The physical led to a sleep test—one I had failed miserably.

Now, I have been fortunate in my career to have been exposed to many world-class people who were also leaders in their respective fields, experts whose opinions influence and shape decisions and policies which affect many. But so far, none had the impact on me this physician had, because this time it was personal.

"Mr. Wyatt, how much sleep do you get on average?"

I replied proudly, "One of my strengths is I don't need a lot of sleep; I get about four to five hours a night and that is all I need."

"No, Mr. Wyatt, you may be getting only four to five hours a night, but you and everyone else in the world needs at least seven to eight hours. The reason you are only sleeping four to five hours a night is because you have sleep apnea, in an extreme form that is having an adverse effect on your health. If you treated your sleep apnea, you would sleep for seven to eight hours on average. I guarantee it."

Irritated, I responded, "I haven't time to sleep for seven or eight hours; I catch up on the weekends!"

"No, you don't; 'catching up' on sleep is not how it works. This is not my opinion; this is science and we have proven it." *Checkmate!*

What I didn't tell you is that my wife was sitting next to me, across from the good doctor. I turned to her and saw "the look," the one that makes me uncomfortable. The look that said either I would be honest with him or she would. I turned sheepishly back to the doctor, surrendered, and said, "Okay, what do you want me to do?"

He prescribed a CPAP machine and that night, for the first time in almost twenty years, I slept eight hours straight; in fact, I slept over nine and a half hours. When I awoke and felt so strange, I was concerned there was something wrong. I called Mayo and described my symptoms, and the physician's assistant I spoke with said, "Mr. Wyatt, this is what you feel like when you are well rested; since it has been years, it may take you some time to get used to this feeling."

The Value of Margin

I was surprised to find that though allowing time to sleep for eight hours cut three to four hours out of my day, my effectiveness increased almost immediately, making the hours I worked more productive. Rather than taking margin from my life, sleep gave it to me. It taught me this lesson: margin makes leadership effective.

In his book, *Margin,* Richard A. Swenson, M.D. begins chapter one, "The conditions of modern day living devour margin." Margin is vital if your leadership is to have impact, and pro leadership requires it.

As I have conducted research in the art of leadership, there is one common thread among people who lead at a high level; they have built margin into their lives. Yes, they built it. None I have read about or interviewed were born with, as Thoreau said, a broad margin; rather, they realized that to be an effective leader they were required to develop and prioritize margin.

Here is a simple example you know, the pre-flight instructions you hear before every commercial flight: "Before helping others, put your own oxygen mask on first." It is the truth; you cannot help others unless you help yourself. Think of margin as your oxygen mask, a basic example of the principle of excavation before elevation: help yourself first, lead yourself first. Only by doing so are you then able to help others; only by doing so will your leadership have impact.

What is margin? It is space, it is a broad shoulder on the road of your life, and not only does it give leadership impact, but also it gives leadership life, because it first gives the leader life. A margin-filled life will help you to inspire and equip the people you lead.

Question: Does your life lack margin, and if so, how can you create it? To begin to answer the question, let's look at life without margin and then to how margin can be created and restored.

What It Looks Like to NOT Have Margin

Pro leadership requires balance and margin in five areas of one's life: physical, mental, emotional, spiritual, and relational-social. I would say that life without margin is pervasive in our culture today and it is killing leadership potential. But since it is not my desire to "pile on" or to shame anyone, rather to inspire and equip, the example I will set forth of a life without margin is my former life, a life that *lacked* margin in each of these five areas, which robbed my leadership of impact. Here is a snapshot of a typical week in my life, before I realized my own lack of margin was making my leadership ineffective:

Monday, 4:45 a.m. My alarm announced the beginning of another week. I showered, shaved, finished packing, had a cup of coffee, and waited for my ride to the airport to arrive at 5:45 a.m. During the twenty-five-minute ride to the airport, I checked my email, giving a quick, four-line read to emails, deleting or forwarding those that needed action by others or flagging those needing my attention. At the airport, I stopped at McDonald's for the perfect meal: an Egg McMuffin and an orange juice. Then, I went into the Delta Sky Club for a cup of coffee and a quick scan of the headlines, before stuffing the *Wall Street Journal* and the local paper into my briefcase to read later. Heading for the gate, I stopped at Starbucks for another coffee to bring on the plane with me. The first flight to New York departed at 7:00 a.m. every Monday, and for five years I was a passenger nearly every week.

7:00—9:00 a.m. The two-hour flight was my time to prepare for the week ahead, and like nearly everyone else on the flight,

I did just that. Bose headphones, the universal "do not disturb" sign, kept my neighbors away. As I look back, I never minded those flights because they actually gave me margin. I could read, I could think, and I could dream—three critical components of margin and impactful leadership.

9:00 a.m.—6:00 p.m. However, that margin ended when the plane's wheels hit the runway at LaGuardia. My executive assistant watched my flight and my phone normally lit up the moment I took it out of airplane mode. In the car on the way to my office in mid-town Manhattan, I was on the phone, first with my assistant, then with one of my partners or senior leaders. Arriving at the office, the race began, weekly one-on-ones with my senior leaders and staff, conference calls, and other "CEO" calls with partners, clients, and top prospects. Normally, it was 6:00 p.m. before I had a minute to think and reflect on the day. But, it was not for long, because most weeks, a dinner meeting ended my day.

All day, every day. During that time, eighteen-hour days were the rule, not the exception—at least three to four days a week. This was my routine for nearly five years. I was in my office in New York three days and sometimes four, returning home either Wednesday or Thursday evening, depending on what needed my presence in New York or Minneapolis. Friday was a catch-up day, a day to tee up the next week so that we could repeat the frenetic pace my role required. I took pride in my ability to run long and fast; but I didn't understand the toll the marginless life was having on me and my leadership.

This lack of margin spilled over to my weekends and my family time. Because I rarely had time to myself, I needed my weekends to catch up. But, like I have been taught that one doesn't catch up on sleep, I've also learned you can't catch up on relationships on the weekends. Rather, the unbalanced pace of life simply spills over, and stress increases as important relationships take a back seat to the need for personal time to recover.

The evidence of a life without margin was manifested in all five of the areas of my life: physical, mental, emotional, spiritual, and social-relational. Physically, I was overweight and out of shape, I looked ten years older than my chronological age. Mentally and emotionally I was fatigued and not sharp, impatient and generally crabby most of the time—all symptoms of running too fast for too long. Spiritually, I was out of touch—empty. I was a living example of what Jesus said, "What good is it to gain the whole world, if you lose your soul?" Socially-relationally, from my closest relationships outward all suffered, because I just did not have the bandwidth to give what was needed.

Today, when I coach leaders, I always smile when they tell me, "It's not the quantity of time but the quality of time that matters in relationships." I used to believe that lie. Now I know that in relationships, there will not be quality time unless there is first quantity of time and attention.

You may be experiencing some discomfort and conviction; you can relate because either this is your life or the life of someone with whom you have a close relationship. Again, this is not a shame chapter, rather I have tried to be generally specific as I relate my story to you as an example of one without margin. I know now my story is not unique, especially today. Swenson wrote *Margin* in 1992, and his lead words are even more true today, "The conditions of modern day living devour margin."

So How Can We Find (and Live with) Margin?

Countless high-impact leaders live lives filled with margin. How did they get there? Where does margin come from and how does a leader create it or restore it if it has been lost?

Like anything leadership-related, to change requires vision, and vision requires desire. Vision and desire must be followed by execution, or, as Albert Einstein said, "Vision without execution is fantasy." Before execution, you must have assessment and development of a plan. To put it in leader terms, you need a strategy and tactics to achieve your goal.

There is a joke told in coaching circles: how many coaches does it take to change a light bulb? The answer: one, but the light bulb must desire to be changed!

If this challenge is resonating, you are probably considering the margin of or lack of margin in your life, and you desire to 1) protect what you have, 2) create additional, or 3) restore what was lost. Like anything else, begin by assessing where you are today. But don't beat yourself up; that is not what this exercise is about. I understand it is hard to look at margin, especially if you don't have it. Writing this chapter and revisiting my past to wade through my marginless life again was no fun. But, in the end, I see that season of my life with clearer eyes, and if my opening up about it can help you, all the better.

Now, let's walk together through the process of creating and restoring margin.

Step One—Assess

Take a look at the five areas of life requiring margin: physical, mental, emotional, spiritual, relational-social. In your journal, for each area, answer the question, "Do I have margin in this area?" To kick-start the assessment, here are three questions you could ask yourself for each area:

Physical

1. What is my physical condition compared to the average person of my age and how it was five years ago?
2. How much sleep do I get on average?
3. Can I walk three flights of stairs without getting winded or breaking a sweat?

Mental

1. How many books have I read in the last year?
2. What type of mental exercises do I do?
3. When was the last time I learned something new?

Emotional

1. Do you keep a journal and when was the last time you wrote in it?
2. How often do you consider your own feelings and when was the last time you shared them with someone close to you?
3. What makes you feel alive and when was the last time you felt that way?

Spiritual

1. Do you believe in a creator or a higher power?
2. What role does that power have in your life?

3. What helps you to get in touch with your soul and when was the last time you allowed for that?

Relational–Social

1. List the ten most important people in your life.
2. In the last week, month and year, how much time have you spent with each one?
3. If you really need help, who could you count on to help if you called?

Next, grade yourself in each area, from one to five or A to F, then figure out your grade-point average. Now, a challenge, share your assessment with someone who loves and cares about you, someone who knows you. See if they agree; talk it over. It may hurt at first, but the outcome will be good, I guarantee it.

Step Two—Make a plan

For each area needing growth, write down a goal for what margin would look like in this area of your life. Here is an example for each:

Physical—run a half-marathon

Mental—read one book a week

Emotional—at the end of each day for the next month I will write in my journal and answer three questions about my day: 1) what did I do right? 2) What would I do differently and 3) what would I change?

Spiritual—For the next month, I will wake up ten minutes early and spend that time feeding my spirit through prayer, meditation and reading.

Relational–Social—For the next three months, I will reserve a breakfast or a lunch each week to give to one of my top ten relationships.

Step Three—Develop Tactics

For your **physical** goal, find a half-marathon running plan. For your **mental** goal, develop a reading list and designate a specific time and place each day to read. For your **emotional** goal, get a journal and before you head to bed, sit down with it for fifteen minutes and some inspiring spiritual reading material and place it in your favorite morning spot, then set your alarm ten minutes early. And for your **relational-social** goal, reach out (e.g., send a text), something like this: "You have been on my mind; would you like to grab breakfast or lunch in the next couple of weeks?"

Step Four—Work Your Plan

Just do it. Execute your plan. Before you know it, margin will become a reality in your life, and its benefits will add impact to your leadership. Like so much in life, growth comes a little bit at a time. The more you think in terms of margin the better you will be at not only building it into your life, but protecting what you have.

The biggest impact margin will have on your life and your leadership is as a stress reducer. Margin is space, in all areas; room to move, the ability to be flexible. Margin gives leadership power; it gives leadership impact. Margin makes leadership effective.

One final thought. You have just completed a chapter on margin, yet nothing was said of money. When I first discuss margin with my clients, without exception money is what they think I am referring to. I was the same way. I had a significant financial margin and believed that took care of it. However, as you read, experience taught me there are more important areas in life requiring margin. So, I will leave the teaching on financial margin to others, such as Dave Ramsey, Susie Orman, Robert Kiyosaki, or your financial advisor, because I realize that if you build margin into the five areas we covered, financial margin may well take care of itself. In other words, financial margin can be a natural outcome of a margin-filled life.

Furthermore, building margin may require you to release some of your expectations and habits in other areas of your life, so that you may simplify your life. For you, it may not be money; it may be your to do list, your calendar, or any action or attitude you believe you can control—that is, in fact, controlling—you. Identify these things and you will find margin and margin is magic, because it makes your leadership effective and that creates impact.

Principle Application

1. How would you define a life with margin?

2. How much margin do you have in your life?

3. If you could add margin, where would you add it?

4. How does your amount of margin affect your ability to lead?

20 | The Wisdom to Diversify

*"Divide your portion to seven, or even to eight,
for you do not know what misfortune may occur on the earth."*
—King Solomon

> **PRO LEADERSHIP PRINCIPLE:** A one-product company is great when it works, but bad when it doesn't.

Medtronic (MDT) is a company I consider the epitome of diversification. It started in the garage of its founder, Earl Bakken, an engineer who developed the first external, wearable pacemaker. In Medtronic's early days, one of my Dad's buddies wrote Earl checks to help him keep going, and in return, they got stock.

One of those friends, a physician I know, gave him five thousand dollars in 1957—a huge investment back then. However, today that man is ninety-seven, and that five thousand investment is now worth over six million dollars! (As an aside, the return on his investment was not his only or even his most impactful benefit. But the bigger truth is that the reason his investment grew by 1200 times is because MDT and its products have saved the lives of countless people all around the world. It is a magnificent humanitarian story—one that I will always use when asked to talk about the benefits of the free market and capitalism.) But, back to diversification.

Success bred success at MDT, allowing it to diversify from just pacemakers. They leveraged the expertise gained in the development of the pacemaker into other life-saving medical products. And, that is how a one-product company became a diversified company. Medtronic is not only known for the impact it has made in the medical-device industry, but also for the impactful leadership of its company. Wise leadership decisions led to wise diversification, allowing leadership to have greater and greater impact.

Learn from Experience

As John Maxwell says, "Sometimes you win, sometimes you learn."

My vision for the business I was building—to be a diversified, world-class investment management firm with global capabilities—if fulfilled, would have produced a well-diversified company able to operate in multiple environments. It was not a unique vision, but a good one, and from where we were, it was quite doable. For us, all it would take was the right people, right philosophy, right process and, of course, right performance (and profit). I like to refer to these as the "4 Ps" of a successful investment firm, or any other business for that matter.

However, when success distracted us from our greater vision, it caused me to take my eyes off diversifying the business. Instead of pouring all of our resources into where we were winning—our fastest growing product—I allowed our single focus to lead the business into a weakened position.

As an investment decision, it was the right thing to do. As Warren Buffett said, "Wide diversification is only required when investors do not understand what they are doing." We knew what we were doing, but although a single focus was the correct investment decision, it was a poor business one. As a leader, I forgot that great investment and business maxim: "Bulls make money, bears make money, but pigs (greedy investors) get slaughtered."

But our large-cap growth business was on a roll. Desiring to take advantage of that success, I sold our private-wealth management business—the foundation of the firm. Then, we hit a rough patch in our hedge fund business, and rather than fix it, and make the changes necessary, I got rid of it. My justification for making these two moves was reasonable. Our largest clients had hired us because we had proven our success as a large-cap growth manager; we reasoned that if they believed we were distracted by these other businesses, products, services, and strategies, they might leave us, and we could not afford that. The more we talked about it, the more we convinced ourselves that our efforts to diversify were, in fact, distractions that had to go. I was wrong to allow myself to be convinced of this.

The decision we made to divest our two other businesses made us a one-trick pony, and that was great, when everything was up and to the right. But, when times changed and our large-cap growth strategy stopped working, those clients we were so intent on pleasing left us. Although they said they were sorry to do so, I don't think they felt half as badly as we did.

Like Wilbur Ross so famously said, "I learned to make good decisions by making bad ones." Once again, I had an opportunity to sit down at my desk, pull out that yellowed legal pad, and write another principle: a one-product company is great when it works, but bad when it doesn't.

Diversification vs. Distraction

Now, let's be real; no one has ever started a diversified company, but many have been built, for the simple fact that you never know what the future will bring. And, as King Solomon—purportedly the world's wisest man—wrote a few millennia ago *"Divide your portion to seven, or even to eight, for you do not know what misfortune may occur on the earth."*

Buffett, too, may be correct about not diversifying your investments, but at the same time, he has built his company, Berkshire Hathaway, into an excellent example of diversification. While diversification will allow a leader like Buffet to have impact, it is important to understand the difference between good business diversification and distraction. As an entrepreneur, it is critical to keep your eye on the ball—*your* ball. You must "do what you do best and hire the rest." I have had countless experiences with brilliant entrepreneurs who were too smart to get out of their own way. They allowed themselves to be distracted, took their eye off the product that got them there in the first place, and the business suffered for it. In some cases, the business ended because of it.

The question is, how does the entrepreneur avoid becoming a business failure statistic? It's simple, but not easy. It's a balancing act, a tension to manage, a dance. Pro leaders stick to the business that made them successful, but they always keep one eye on the future. Many great companies commit a certain percentage of revenue or earnings to research and development—that is a great idea. Even as a start-up, you must consider product improvement—thinking down the road and around the corner. Read Walter Isaacson's biography of Steve Jobs; although he was a once-in-a-generation entrepreneur, we can learn from him. He always had one eye on the future, and it paid off, big time.

One of the problems with a start-up is typically scarce resources, which leads to the attitude of, "We will spend money on research and development when . . ." The problem is that "when" rarely comes because the urgent so often keeps us from the important. But, as the leader, you need to find a way.

One of the best ways I have found is to do research and development and to read widely. I am not talking about industry pieces—I am talking about a well-rounded reading plan, across all disciplines. My goal is to read a minimum of forty-five minutes a day. Once I set that goal, it is amazing how often I ended up reading for an hour or more. My reading plan is simple, I read in five areas: History/Biography, Business/Current Affairs, Personal Development, Spiritual Development, and Literature/Fiction/Fun. I generally have five books going at a time, one from each category. Reading stimulates creativity a key to any leader's success—plus, you never know where a new idea will come from (an idea that may lead to further diversification!).

I am around a lot of leaders, and I always feel bad when I hear someone say, "I am too busy to read." My answer is, "I'm too busy not to read." As John Maxwell said, "Leaders are readers." I agree. Doing so will keep both you and your company fresh.

If you are leading a one-product company, that's great. As my Dad used to say, "You must dance with the one you brought to the dance." Make that product great, but don't forget the downside of a one-product company. Take steps to diversify: budget for research and development, form a mastermind group to explore ways to diversify your business and to think about the future and how your business will prosper in it. Start small and think big. Your budget does not need to be anything more than your time—in the beginning. Do it; you won't regret it.

Think of your business as an investment portfolio; no wise investor will put all their eggs in one basket. Remember, one-product companies are great when they work, and bad when they don't.

How to "Research and Develop"

Begin your own R&D project to help you consider how to diversify. Set aside a block of time to assess your business: your product or service, your revenue sources, your industry. Don't allow yourself to be pulled into the weeds, this is not an exercise in financial modeling. Neither is this a left-brain exercise. This is a creative exercise meant for your right brain. Now, answer these questions, and add some more of your own:

1. What business are we in?
2. In the beginning how/why did we choose this business?
3. Why would someone choose us over someone else?
4. What do we do best?
5. What can we do better than anyone else?
6. Can this skill be used for anything else?
7. Where is our industry going?
8. What will we need to do in order to remain competitive?
9. How much time will it take?

10. How much time do you have?
11. How much will it cost to do?
12. How much will it cost if we don't do it?
13. Do I have the right people?
14. If not, what type of people do we need?
15. If I started over today, what type of business would I start?

If you were my coaching client, I would ask you these questions and help you come to your own answers. As you answered, I would ask clarifying questions in order to help you get to the real answer to the question, often asking it in a different way to help you get to your own deeper truth. Let's consider each question and why its answer is important.

What business are you in? When asked this question, often people will answer with what they do, not with the business they are in. For example, most people will tell you that McDonalds is in the hamburger or the restaurant business, but McDonalds is actually in the real estate business. IBM is another good example. Although they started as a computer manufacturer, and to the average person they are still a computer company, today, IBM is a consulting and Artificial Intelligence (AI) company. It is vital to understand that the business you are in is more than what you do because it is the first step in thinking outside of your "box." The first step is confronting any limiting beliefs currently keeping you and your business from its highest and best.

In the beginning how/why did we choose this business? None of us can see the future, however, our history will help us see how we got to where we are today and help us understand our tendencies and biases which will influence our future. As Mark Twain said, "History doesn't repeat itself, but it often rhymes." Knowing where the business came from will help you understand how you got to this place today and if your current trajectory continues, where you may be tomorrow. Sometimes a business needs to go back to its beginnings in order to refresh its future.

Why would someone choose us over someone else? What is your unique value proposition? Answering this question will boost your leadership confidence. It helps you to focus on what matters most: the 20 percent that will contribute 80 percent of your impact. Coming to an honest answer of this question will also help you to see where improvements may need to be made.

What do we do best? This question is the company version of "Who am I?" What are you best at, where do you win? The answer will help you to sharpen your focus and you consider the future. Sometimes, my clients will come to the realization the market or their clients have pushed them away from their highest and best. As a result, they become better equipped to make a necessary course correction.

What can we do better than anyone else? This may sound like a repeat of the last question, but it is not. You may identify your best, but if best is not better than your competitors, you will struggle to win. This is a gut-check question. I have had clients tell me what they do better than anyone, but realize they are not doing it. My question back to them is, "Have you ever considered selling consulting services to help your clients become more efficient?" There may be a diversified revenue source they'd not considered before.

Can this skill be used for anything else? This is a follow-on to the last two questions. What skill is this, and can it be used in any way other than how you are using it today, and could that become another source of revenue?

Where is our industry going? No one knows the future. But pro leaders think about it and develop an outlook. They also know to treat their outlook like perfume; smell it, don't swallow it. It is good practice to develop two or three scenarios and to think each through to the end.

What will we need to do in order to remain competitive? For each of your scenarios, consider how your company would be positioned if you made no adjustments, then sketch out what would need to change for you to continue to prosper in each case.

How much time will it take? If you need to make changes or adjustments, how quickly can you do it? How fast can you get to market?

How much time do you have? How fast are your market, your industry, or your competitors moving? Each of your scenarios will have a time horizon, what is it?

How much will it cost to do? Don't cost account at this point. You want a ballpark estimate. As the leader, your estimate will be directionally correct and good enough for now.

How much will it cost if we don't do it? This is a value question. Some people know the cost of everything but the value of nothing. I have coached leaders who are so fixed on the cost that they risk the entire value of the enterprise because they miss the big picture. To consider this is wise.

Do I have the right people? To borrow from Jim Collins, who wrote *Good to Great*, in order to go where you will need to go with your business, do you have the right people on the bus and are they in the right seats? If the answer is no, don't panic, or if the answer is yes, don't get proud. The truth is probably somewhere in the middle, and time will help you to deal with that. Today's answer is more about your own awareness as a leader than about making immediate changes.

If not, what type of people do we need? If you need to change your people, what do they need to change to? Whom do you need?

If I started over today, what type of business would I start or buy? It is good to end with a gut check. Are you in a good business? Do you want to continue; is the opportunity still there to win? You have only one life, is this where you want to spend it? Don't fear your answer; if you know the truth, the truth will set you free.

Done completely and well, this is a half-day exercise. Get away, get alone, get relaxed, and go for it—your answers may surprise you. Your next step is to lead your leadership team through these same questions. But, don't share your answers until the end. This is an impactful exercise that will turbo-charge your team and your leadership and it will help you as you diversify your company.

Completing this exercise will inspire and encourage you in your leadership because it will affirm your "Why." It will clarify your mission, give focus to your strategy and your tactics, and empower your leadership with greater impact.

Principle Application

1. As a leader, what do you do best?

2. What does your company or organization do best?

3. What do you see as the biggest risk to your company or organization?

4. What do you see as the biggest risk to your leadership?

5. How can you mitigate these risks?

21 | The 45-Minute Meeting

"Meetings are usually terrible, but they shouldn't be."
—Patrick Lencioni

> **PRO LEADERSHIP PRINCIPLE:** The majority of any meeting's benefit is realized in the first forty-five minutes.

Covert Baily, in his book, *Fit or Fat?*, expounded on the benefits of aerobic exercise, and explained the science supporting his statement that 85 percent of the benefit of aerobic exercise is realized in the first twenty minutes. Any time spent exercising after those first twenty minutes, while beneficial, has a diminishing return. His premise is that everyone who can find twenty minutes a day for aerobic exercise can go from "fat to fit."

The same is true of meetings; the majority of any meeting's benefit is realized in the first forty-five minutes. After that, the meeting's returns diminish. My therapist taught me this. I will never forget my first appointment with her—a wonderful woman who helped me get to the bottom of "what's bugging me." It was supposed to be an hour-long appointment, but fifty minutes in, she looked up at me and said, "I think we are done for today. I will see you next week." And just like that, she showed me out the door. As I left, I heard her greet her next client.

Being the very average, very type-A American male that I am, it took forty-five years and one really hard push from my wife to schedule that session. I'd just assumed that talk therapy was a waste of time! It wasn't until I tried it for myself that I realized it would have a positive, lasting effect on my life. Her therapy was not only good for me personally, but also for my business and my life. In fact, it was this same therapist who taught me one important pro leadership principle: the majority of any meeting's benefit is realized in the first forty-five minutes.

I didn't understand it at the moment, but now I see why she showed me the door ten minutes early. She didn't want to waste anyone's time. She understood the value of time, that it cannot be managed but only spent, so to maximize its benefits you must manage yourself.

Death by Meeting

Let's be honest, some types of meetings require significantly more time than forty-five minutes, such as strategic meetings like board meetings, annual planning meetings, etc. But even those, I have learned, are simply a number of smaller meetings on a single "agenda," and rarely does a single agenda item require more than forty-five minutes. Few people can or should sit any longer–the Apple watch has taught us all that. *Time to stand!*

I remember telling a friend of mine, "I think my dog has attention deficit disorder" (my friend happened to be our dog's veterinarian).

"Well, of course he does," my friend the vet replied. "All dogs do, as do most entrepreneurs, CEOs, and high-level leaders."

If that's true (and I'm inclined to believe it is), that's why so many of us can relate to Patrick Lencioni's book *Death by Meeting.* This book helped me transform the culture of my company. Not only did it change the way I thought about meetings in general, but it helped reinforce the wisdom of the forty-five-minute meeting rule, and develop it as a Pro Leadership principle.

For one, I have learned to write—and do anything else creative—in the morning. I am at my best when I first wake up. I have learned that I can focus well for up to ninety minutes at a time when I am alone, but in any meeting—any meeting—you will lose me after forty-five.

However, this part is critical: if you want to make the forty-five-minute meeting rule work for you in your workplace, you must follow some guidelines. Those guidelines are: be on time, be prepared, be current, start with the end in mind, and know the desired outcome of the meeting—and get there.

How to Run Productive Meetings

First, be on time. Timeliness is like a muscle: the more you use it, the stronger it will become. At one point in my life, I was chronically late. Like so many of life's lessons, I learned the hard way to be on time.

Because my home is in Minneapolis, a Delta hub, I am a Delta frequent flyer. I have spent over two thousand hours sitting in an airplane seat in the air (and that does not count ground time or airport time). There was a time when people would ask me what "status" I had on Delta, and I would tell them, "Idiot—it's after Diamond." Then I told them I had a special relationship with Delta, and they would ask, "What is that?"

"If I'm not there, they leave without me," I would respond. This always got a laugh—everyone could relate to it. Many of them also had that special relationship, not only with Delta, but also with United and American and Alaska!

Golf has taught me a similar lesson. Tee times are not loose; 8:10 means 8:10—if you're not there, they have no problem taking you out to your group, which can mean missing a hole or two. When I played golf in high school, we were required to be at the first tee ten minutes before our tee time, or we would be penalized. This is a good lesson I aim to apply in life: be ready for the meeting ten minutes before it's scheduled to start. This allows time for your brain to refocus and transition you to the next task. Time is margin, and margin—as we have learned—helps all leaders to be at their best. Margin will help you be prepared and preparation is a key to an effective meeting.

Be prepared. Know the purpose of the meeting and have a draft agenda. I say "draft," because you need to be flexible and open to discussing a need that may not be on the docket. It is paramount to build margin/whitespace into every agenda, because you just don't know what may come up! In my leadership beginnings, I considered all meetings "my meeting." Later, as a wise leader, I changed my mind and now consider all one-on-one meetings "their meeting." Yes, I have a loose agenda, but my most critical role is encouragement and coaching, and I believe that should be the case for all leaders.

The meeting before the meeting is often the best way to be prepared. I learned this from a mentor who was also an outside director of a board I chaired. One week prior to our board meetings he would call me to review the meeting's agenda and to ask me any questions he had. If he wasn't comfortable with my answers he would say so, giving me an opportunity to clarify or to strengthen my answers. Then, at the board meeting he would ask the same questions again, allowing me to answer them again, this time, in a clearer and more focused way.

Time does not always allow for a meeting before every meeting, but as the leader, you will benefit greatly by discussing meeting goals and objectives, with the key participants of the meeting, before it takes place. This is another way to ensure margin because it gives your players time to think about the issues to be addressed outside of the natural pressure of the meeting.

Meeting prep conversations may easily be had as a part of any leader's "management by walking around." While checking in with your team, it is natural to ask a question about an upcoming meeting. Something like this: "I know we are meeting tomorrow with so and so, on such and such. What would you like the outcome of the meeting to be? What can I do to help the goal to be accomplished?" Any meeting before a meeting will not only prepare you but you will also be current—a vital ingredient in preparation.

Be current. Solomon wrote, "A good shepherd knows the condition of his flock." As a leader, I have come to appreciate the importance of knowing what is going on in the lives of my associates. In the past, I have asked countless people, "How are you?" and then not listened to their answer. Today, I know not to ask the question if I am not willing to take the time to listen to the answer. For me, the best way to stay current was my daily walk around the office—the tactic I call "management by walking around."

In the beginning, when we were a four-person company, I spoke to each of my three associates each day. As we grew, that was not always possible, but I made sure I at least acknowledged every associate every single day. But every day that I was in one of our offices, I made sure that I stopped in to "chat" with my team leaders. The natural outcome of those casual encounters was increased efficiency and productivity in their weekly meetings, because I already knew what was going on in their lives. It allowed me the time to ask the most important question a leader asks . . . "How can I help?"

Know what your desired outcome is; begin with the end in mind. Stephen Covey, in his book *Seven Habits of Highly Successful People,* taught to begin with the end in mind. I learned to do that long before I read Covey's book. My dad often said, "If you don't know where you are going, you won't like where you end up." When it comes to the objective of a meeting, nothing truer has ever been said. The leader's role is to determine beforehand what the objective of the meeting is, and then make sure it gets there before it ends. In this way, every meeting is a "crucial conversation," what I call "speaking the last 10 percent."

This is often the hardest part, as it is the implementation of your leadership role. It is like this: most people will speak to an issue up to the point where they become uncomfortable, because they are worried that they will offend or make another uncomfortable. As a rule, I have found it is the last 10 percent of a conversation that often creates "waves." Waves make many seasick, so they don't want to "make any waves." However, it is often the last 10 percent of a conversation— that part that makes waves—that provides the breakthrough needed for progress.

So, as the leader, it is important to recognize where the point of discomfort is with an issue and make sure that point is hit. It is the responsibility of leadership to make sure all critical points, good or bad, are covered—regardless of any emotions stirred up making the point.

This is where a leader's level of emotional intelligence is crucial. It is your EI that gives you the ability to read the room and to control the tone of the meeting, so that even the difficult-to-discuss, more emotional issues may be handled in a way that is respectful to all who are involved. A leader who creates a culture where difficult issues can be discussed in a safe and respectful manner will not only build a following, but will also lead with impact.

Be disciplined. Finally, a few tactics that will provide practical discipline, adding to the effectiveness of any leader, are:

1) Calendar the hour, even though you manage the meeting to forty-five minutes. Doing so will add margin to your day by giving you time to reflect after a meeting or for any "post meeting" crucial conversations. Reflection and relationally valuable conversations are not possible if you are always running to your next meeting.

2) For the same reason, discipline yourself to allow "travel time" between meetings. Resist the temptation to book back-to-back meetings. Even if your next meeting is in the same place as your previous meeting, build in white space; thirty minutes works well. Again, think margin. Effective leadership requires time: time to think, time to reflect, and time to breathe.

Reality Check

One of my favorite shows of all time is *West Wing*. I used to love the energy of the show and imagined myself as President Bartlett, where the only transition between meetings was him saying, "What's next?" It made good TV, but it was leadership fantasy.

Pro leadership is not like that. Effective and impactful leadership requires time, whitespace, and margin. It is true: time cannot be managed, but calendars can. So, take care of yourself, take care of your calendar.

At the end of the day, there is little we can do to eliminate meetings—they are a necessary part of business. But they don't have to be "terrible," and you don't have to experience "death by meeting." Like anything else, you simply need to prepare, and remember: the majority of the benefit of any meeting comes in the first forty-five minutes!

Build a culture of short, efficient meetings and respect your team's time. Your leadership will get easier, and you will have more impact.

Principle Application

1. What do you believe is needed to make a meeting effective?

2. What types of meetings frustrate you and leave you demotivated?

3. What types of meetings encourage you and leave you inspired and enthusiastic?

4. How do you know when a meeting needs to end?

5. What is the most efficient way to use meetings in your leadership?

22 | Embrace Your Failures

"Failures, repeated failures, are fin-
ger posts on the road to achievement.
One fails forward toward success."
—C. S. Lewis

"My failures have made me look at myself in
a way I've never wanted to before."
—Tiger Woods

> **PRO LEADERSHIP PRINCIPLE:** Failures are
> seeds of success.

There are two types of entrepreneurs: those who *have* failed and those who *will* fail. That's why starting over is a skill all entrepreneurs and leaders must master. (As I have throughout this book, I realize I am often using the term "entrepreneur" interchangeably with "leader." You see, I am a leader, but before that, I was an entrepreneur.)

We all must learn how to see our mistakes as a tool that can help us in the future. This principle came to roost for me when, after twenty-four years, the business that I had founded, led, and poured my life into, came to an end. Although it was a necessary ending, it broke my heart. However, the sun rose the next morning, and the morning after that, and slowly but surely, I regained my balance.

Winston Churchill said, "Success is going from failure to failure without loss of enthusiasm." That was me. I had been knocked off my horse and I took it hard. But I didn't stay there. I have learned failure is a part of life—a big part—and it is not the failure that matters. What matters is that you get back up and start again.

It is counterintuitive, but it's very true: the experience of failure can help a leader to have greater impact, if he or she uses that failure wisely. And that impact will be a result of the application of this pro leadership principle: *failures are seeds of success.*

Churchill faced failure and defeated it; it made him who he was and he was intimately familiar with its benefits. After he was elected Prime Minister of Great Britain in May of 1940, while visiting King George VI for the first time, he told the king when asked about the impending German attack, "Countries that fight to the end rise again; countries that surrender never rise again." I love those words and I love that attitude. Never, never, never quit. Churchill's words were true for Great Britain, but they are also true today in both business and life.

When Enough is Enough

Maybe you are experiencing a failure right now, as you read this. Maybe you have failed time and time again. Welcome to the club—you now share something with all great human beings. Failure is a reality of our human experience. The reason we don't remember the failures of great people we admire is because they did not allow their failures to stop them; rather, they learned from them and continued onward to victory and impact.

No leader I have ever met or studied planned to fail. But many plans do fail, so the most important question to answer when a plan goes south is, "When is it time to say 'enough'?" You cannot start over until you stop whatever is not working.

We wrestled with this question for six months before reaching the conclusion that the right thing was to turn out the lights on the company. I will never forget the day. It was a Saturday in October of 2016, and we were in the midst of fighting for our business life. During that time, I was listening to an Audible book while driving, *Necessary Endings* by Henry Cloud. I don't recall the specifics, but I remember having a strong sense that our business' ending was necessary. That is when I first began to think about starting over.

Five months later, twenty-four years after first turning the lights on in that company, I turned them off and stepped from a necessary ending into a new beginning. As time passed, I regained my balance and gained perspective on the twenty-four years spent building my business career. Now, I realize that I have started over many times already, and each time it has led to something better, more fulfilling, and often, more life-giving than what I had done before.

How did I know it was time to stop so that I could begin again? How do I know I wasn't just quitting or giving up too soon? Simple, I didn't know; the tough decisions of leadership, like this one, are rarely black and white; rather shades of grey requiring a leader to stand on experience and knowledge and make the best decision under the circumstances. At the end of the day, it is a "gut" call. Here is what I do know: a good leader will do the right thing and let the chips fall where they may. In my case, I had done everything possible to save the company, exhausting all avenues. The final decision was a human one; to continue would have put the futures of our team at risk, and I could not bring myself to sacrifice the people who had meant so much to me, just to satisfy my own ego. The right thing was to let it go, and I did. It was the most difficult decision I have made, but I learned, just because it's hard doesn't mean it's wrong.

Once a tough decision like this is made, a pro leader seeks to learn the lessons of failure. If you allow it, failure can be a wonderful teacher ultimately launching you to greater heights than you had known before.

Five Questions to Ask after Failure

As a teacher-coach, I have a few simple rules: you can only teach what you have learned, you can only lecture on what you have lived, and you can only proclaim what you have claimed. I lived a business failure and what I learned is this: failures are often the seeds of success.

One of the most important ways to live out this principle is to train yourself to properly reflect on your failure experience, in order to recognize and apply the lessons in it. To do this, I borrow the discipline I learned from my friend and world-class coach, Jay Coughlin. This is the discipline he practiced as a CEO, and which he wrote about in his excellent book *Five Bold Choices*. This discipline includes asking yourself five important questions, which I've shared below with my own answers, for my situation. You can do something similar for your own:

1. **What did I do right?** In my situation, I could see that we gave it enough time to work, after it seemed it had stopped working. All businesses and markets are cyclical, so the critical thing is to make sure the business is actually broken, and it's not just a market cycle or a condition that is going to self-correct and right the business. Secondly, we put our people first, ending while we could still afford to give them time. No one thinks when they put a team together that they will one day have to let them go—but if that day comes, remember, you are dealing with *people*. We wanted to be fair, to be honest and to be gentle. This didn't happen because of them, and we wanted them all to know it.

2. **What would I do differently?** This is the tough one. Hindsight is 20:20, so it's easy to make decisions using the rearview mirror. But knowing what I now know, I would have moved faster to make changes with the broken strategy. I would have started over sooner, and I would have foregone the strategic partnership as it did not give us what we needed. I was wrong to think that bigger would be better. Rather, I should have stuck to my personal philosophy, the one that had served me so well throughout my life: slow and steady wins the race.

3. **What would I change?** Although this sounds like a repeat of the above question, it is not, because I am not able to change everything I would do differently. So, what would I change? I would not be afraid to start over. Mark Twain said it best, "I have spent a lot of my life worrying about a lot of things, most of which have never happened." The asset management business had changed dramatically since I entered it over three

decades earlier. It has always been a tough business, but then, it wasn't just tough, it was changing dramatically.

So, if I could change anything, I would have started over, in another business. I would have started with me. I would have figured out sooner who I am and what is my why. I would have better understood my strengths and tried to find a business where I could apply them.

Here is the thing: I wasn't even asking these questions even ten years ago—I was too busy climbing the ladder of success, only to find out I had it leaning against the wrong building.

I gained a lot of wisdom over those years. I call it my "street MBA," and the lessons I have learned, the ones that are the most valuable, have very little (if anything) to do with the specific business I had built. This wisdom is mostly about people and how to lead them, which is transferrable to the business of life. It is in all the pro leader principles in this book.

Seeds for the Future

I now find myself in the second half of my life, in terms of life span. In the ten years preceding the writing of this book, I was still in the "first half" of my life, and it is not possible to implement second-half strategies when you are still in the first half. Two books and one experience helped me come to terms with being in the second half of life: *Half Time*, by Bob Buford, and *Falling Upward*, by Richard Rohr. These two books helped me to understand that my identity was not the business, and I was more than my accomplishments or, in this case, my failures. I also spent time at a three-day silent retreat at the Jesuit

Retreat House at Demontraville. The combination of these three things, along with time to contemplate the failure of the business, gave me a new perspective and hope that the future could be greater than the past, and to embrace the principle that failures can be the seeds of success.

Please note that I don't necessarily mean that failures are the seeds of *financial* success. Maybe that will be true, maybe not—but I don't care anymore. I have had enough money in my life to have learned it doesn't satisfy. What I mean when I say my future will be "greater" is that I will now be operating out of my essence—as the person I have been created to be, not from some secondary identity. I will be operating out of my primary identity, the true me. A friend gave me a golf ball inscribed with these words, "Be true to your identity. You do *you*!" This ball will never see the course. Rather, it will sit on my desk as a daily reminder of how to be a true success.

Remember, when faced with failure, giving yourself permission to start over is the first thing you have to do. It is hard, and it takes courage, perseverance, and the wisdom and confidence to be discreet about it, because people may not immediately support you in your restart. However, I have learned not to expect overt support right away, or to blame those who are simply too fearful to lend support. I am not a trained psychologist, but I do know people, and I would bet at least 80 percent of the people surrounding us are afraid of failure and would do almost anything to avoid the pain of it. As a result, they may not have any idea how to come alongside someone who is experiencing it. So, don't take it personally.

My experience has taught me the majority of people are so risk averse that they forget to live—they end up merely existing, living for the weekend, for their next vacation, for retirement. And when that happens, they miss the beauty of today. We don't have to live that way.

My failures have taught me many things, but high on the list is this: I have learned to appreciate today, to be where I am, and not to wish the day away. I have learned an attitude of gratitude, since that is where joy comes from. I am not afraid of failure anymore. I was once; in fact, I did a lot of things hoping to avoid it. In hindsight, that avoidance caused much pain and delay of what has turned out to be the best for my life.

If you are in this position now—or if you ever do get into it—I hope you will give yourself permission to start over—and do it. Answer the questions *Who am I?* and *What is my why?* Then, get alone and develop a vision of your life, the way you would live if you were operating out of your essence—being truly yourself.

Next, map out the strategy and the tactics you believe best to get there. Seek counsel, talk to your spouse, meet your mentor, get therapy. Go to your inner circle and to your personal board of directors. Remember what King Solomon said, "Plans fail for lack of counsel."

I was fifty-six years old when my business failed. I lost a great deal, but two valuable things I gained were: 1) the gift of time, and 2) the ability to choose what I wanted to do. Many people asked me, "Are you going to retire?" This was a natural question, since many of my peers were moving in that direction. Not me. I have started over; entrepreneurial DNA doesn't retire; if you have it, it is part of who you are. As they say, "If you're not dead, you're not done!" My "why" is "to inspire and equip leaders who desire to develop the leader within so that they may become all they were created to be." To retire would be to stop doing my why, and that would be to deny who I am.

What the world needs more of is leadership, courage, and character. I want to be part of that and I hope you do, too. So, if and when you experience failure—congratulations because failures are the seeds of success. And, they contribute to one other thing you will need for the journey of pro leadership: perspective—and that is the focus of the next chapter.

Principle Application

1. What does failure feel like to you?

2. How has the experience of a failure made you a more effective leader?

3. When you've been open about your failures, how have those closest to you reacted?

4. How does failure motivate you?

5. Is fear of failure keeping you from doing something you feel called to do? How so?

23 | Major, Don't Minor

"We become what we repeatedly do."
—Stephen Covey

> **PRO LEADERSHIP PRINCIPLE:** Focus on the big picture; what you see is what you will be.

I was flying cross-country once on a wide-body jet, and coincidently, I knew one of the pilots. As we flew, I pondered the responsibility he held as we flew hundred miles an hour at 35,000 feet. Every seat was full and with a full crew there must have been three hundred people on the plane.

A few days later I ran into him and asked, "Do you ever consider the people you have seated behind you and the responsibility you have for their safety?" His response was an example of what I call "majoring on the majors;" he looked at me and smiled, then said, "I never think about the people on the plane. Doing so might distract me from my job. Besides, if I land safely, so do they."

Majoring on the majors doesn't come naturally for most leaders. Rather, doing so is, for most, a learned skill. Some personality types find it more natural and others less so, but the good news is, with discipline and practice, it is a skill that anyone can acquire, build, and strengthen. If you desire to lead with impact, "majoring on the majors" needs to be an essential tool in your leadership toolbox.

Four Examples of What This Looks Like

Example #1: I walked into Dick's office for a daily tutoring session with a master craftsman. His craft was investing, and in his day, there was no one better. It was the mid-eighties and the *Star Wars* movies were enrapturing most everyone. As I waited for Dick to finish his call, I felt like Luke Skywalker waiting for Obi-Wan Kenobi to show up. He hung up, shook his head, and, with a frown, looked at me and said, "Quarterly earnings are the worst thing to ever happen to the investment world. They have created a herd of short-term thinkers, and no one can ever succeed long term with a short-term view."

I wrote that one down, but I didn't need to, because I have never forgotten it. It was a perfect example of majoring on majors and not on minors. The lesson continued when I asked, "Why?" I then received a lecture on how short-term thinking more often than not results in winning a battle but losing a war.

I did not record Dick's lecture, but here are my notes: "It is professional investors who have driven corporations to think short term, quarter-by-quarter, so we have no one to blame but ourselves. Setting investors' responsibility aside, leaders of most publicly-held companies are now managing their businesses for quarterly results, and ninety days is too short a period to gain the perspective needed to make good business decisions."

Example #2: My second lesson on majoring on the majors was from a leader who has built his life and his reputation on his long-term view (i.e., majoring on the majors not on the minors). This friend was the CFO of a public company that Warren Buffett acquired. It was an exciting day for my friend, who relished the opportunity to be part of Buffett's company, Berkshire Hathaway. He was visiting me one day, when I asked him, "How is it going with Warren?"

With a broad smile, he replied, "It's wonderful; we can now make good long-term business decisions instead of having to think in ninety-day blocks of time. Just eliminating the distraction of the quarterly earnings report and calls has allowed us to focus on what matters the most."

I asked him to give me an example. "Last week we finished our first quarter as part of Berkshire Hathaway," he said, "so I called Warren's office and left a message that I wanted to schedule a meeting to review the quarter with him. Less than an hour later, my phone rang, and it was Warren. He asked me if there was something wrong. I said no, but that I'd just thought he would like to review the quarter."

He said that Warren laughed and said, "Jim, we bought you not for this quarter, but for forever, so unless there is a problem that is going to keep you from succeeding long term, we don't need to talk. You have better things to do than talk to me." That is majoring on majors—and there is no better example of that than Warren Buffett.

Example #3: This one was personal. When we entered into our strategic partnership with a large financial services firm, as a subsidiary we became part of their planning and reporting cycle. It was a three-year rolling plan, updating and rolling every quarter. On paper it looked like a brilliant tool, straight out of a top-tier business school. In practice, it failed because of the way it rolled every ninety days.

By the second quarter, we realized it was not really a three-year plan, but a ninety-day plan. The plan became paramount and all decision-making had to fit into it. Every decision came down to—how would it affect the plan, today. This slowed the pace of the business, causing missed opportunities and negative long-term results.

For a cost accountant, a three-year plan with a ninety-day roll is a wonderful tool, but for a leader it forces a focus on cost. This leads to missing opportunities that create real value. Having experienced a large organization like this, I can understand how it can get to this type of planning and reporting but can also see the negative effect this "majoring on minors" (in this case, ninety-day periods), can have on a business and on its leaders. No leader can have impact while majoring on minors.

Example #4: "People" are where leaders often get caught majoring on minors and our fourth example touches on this problem. Hired to develop the middle market for an established company, a man I know was hired for his people skills and his ability to close. Young and successful in his previous sales position, the only risk in bringing him on was the product and industry he had successfully sold in was not the one this company expected him to conquer. He had the intangibles; his boss told him he had hired for talent, not position. He would teach him that. So off he went. The sales cycle was longer here, in this new world, than what he had experienced, and it would test his metal. Nine months in, nothing. A lot of relationships, but no new revenue.

His sales manager grew frustrated, believing he had been right in objecting to the CEO's hiring for talent. He was called in to his sales manager's office. "You have ninety days; either you meet your numbers or you're gone. I guess it was just too big of a leap to go from computer sales to this."

Gulp! The young man went to his mentor and asked, "What do I do?"

The wise one replied, "Keep doing what you have been doing. Relationship sales take time. You'll be fine, whatever happens."

On day eighty-five, the young sales guy was having lunch with one of his prospects, who mentioned that they were considering hiring his firm to manage pension assets. He responded honestly, "I'm sorry, I won't get to work with you."

Mr. Prospect asked, "Why?"

"I have only five days to meet my quota or I am going to be fired," he told the client.

"I'm sorry to hear that," said Mr. Prospect. "What is your quota?"

"It's an impossible number—thirteen million dollars."

His prospect smiled but didn't say another word, only promised he would call on day ninety and check in. He did call on day ninety and said that his company was going to put thirteen million dollars with him on one condition: that he be allowed to stay! That is the short story of my first year in the investment management industry, a career that lasted thirty-three years.

In the short term, the hiring seemed wrong, but long term it was right. With people, time is the difference between majoring and minoring—to major takes time and patience.

Four Realities

With every example of a principle comes a reality. Understanding the realities of the examples cited above will help you to major on the majors and move you off the minors, if you find yourself stuck there. Looking at these realities can help you as you face your own examples and come to terms with their unique realities. (Remember as you do that realities are more often than not tensions to manage rather than problems to be solved.)

Example #1 Reality (Obi-Wan's Lesson to Me, Young Luke Skywalker, on the Downfall of Quarterly Earnings): Recognize the short-term nature of quarterly business thinking. The reality here is that quarterly thinking is the direct outcome of the increasing speed of business. As a direct result of the "Amazonization" of everything, as a culture we have become accustomed to having almost everything be "just in time," which really means, *I want it now*. This global impatience is a manifestation of the greed and fear that are two basic drivers of human behavior. These behaviors have been with us since the beginning of creation; they won't be solved and must be managed. To do so we must discipline ourselves to think long term.

Example #2 Reality (Warren Buffett's Epic Response to My Friend's Phone Call). Recognize the wisdom of taking a long-term view. Buffett has always taken a long-term view. The wisdom of this approach has not always been obvious, but in hindsight it is. As I mentioned earlier, the problem with this life is we live it forward but understand it backwards.

The business he has built allows Buffett to take the long-term perspective, a perspective gained from the diversification and margin, resulting from the long-term success of his value-based philosophy. His long-term view allows him to have . . . a long-term view; success has bred success.

Example #3 Reality (The Failure of the Three-Year Plan with the Ninety-Day Roll) Recognize that risk management drives short-term thinking. The reality here is that businesses must manage risk, and the bigger the enterprise, the bigger the risks.

Business schools teach and preach risk management. An inordinate focus on risk drives a certain type of decision-making, which leads to majoring on minors instead of majors. In every business that experiences great success, there is a point at which the total enterprise becomes the priority over any one particular venture or initiative. This may be one of the reasons growth slows; you cannot score on defense. This may also be why a small, nimble company often has an advantage over a large company.

Example #4 Reality (How I Nearly Lost My Investment Career before It Even Started) Recognize it takes time to develop talent. The time/talent reality is a tension that is a big part of any growth company. The smaller the company, the smaller the headcount, and the less leadership is able to be patient developing talent.

Everyone must pull their weight, today—if they don't the organization feels it. In a large company, with many employees they have the ability to take time to develop talent, because one person's work is a smaller percentage of the whole compared to the same person's work in a small company. So, the reality in a small firm is that the commitment to *take time to develop talent* must be clearly understood when hiring anyone. The alternative to time is to hire for position, but this can be expensive; although you may hire competence, you have no guarantee of character.

As you personally consider where you could be "majoring on the majors," I encourage you to clearly examine the realities of your own examples. Next, let's apply wisdom to the four examples. (To get the most out of an experience, to have it influence your judgment and result in wisdom, it must be *applied*.)

Four Ways to Apply Wisdom

Wisdom Applied from Example #1: Clearly short-term thinking has a place in business. This is a good place to apply the 80:20 principle—80 percent long term, 20 percent short term.

Every leader's day is filled with two types of issues: urgent and important. That's the way life is. The key, as Stephen Covey wrote, is not to allow the urgent to displace the important. In the same manner, strategic decisions are important, while tactical ones are often urgent. Manage these tensions using the 80:20 rule, and you will naturally develop a habit of majoring on the majors, because your energies will be going to long-term, important, and strategic efforts. This will assure you are leading with impact.

Wisdom Applied from Example #2. Buffett's wisdom is the result of holding to his long-term view. Any leader can do the same, but to do so requires three specific actions on your part:

1. you must know who you are; and who you're not
2. you must know your why
3. you must think inside out

Inside-out decision-making results from knowing and being comfortable with who you are, together with knowing your why. This will lead you to become a long-term decision-maker and thinker. As a result, your leadership will be impactful.

Wisdom Applied from Example #3. You cannot die on every mountain. Understand what can be changed and what cannot. Majors can be changed, minors cannot. Every company has a personality and a constitution. Don't try to fight it; rather understand it and determine how you can use it and leverage it to maximize your leadership. Major on the things you can affect and spend little time if any on the things you cannot. Doing so will give your leadership impact.

Wisdom Applied from Example #4. Hire talent 80 percent and position 20 percent. Many factors make or break a hire, but two factors more than anything determine long-term success: character and competence. Major on character and competence, this is the key to winning the people battle.

My grandfather pioneered the practice of pediatric surgery on newborns and infants in the United States. He hired and trained the first group of surgeons in this field. As a pioneer, he couldn't hire for position, so he chose character and competence. These were the people who ultimately perfected the practice.

It is much the same in a growth business, where members of the team are often required to wear multiple hats. Character and competence are often better able to adjust, while position players are often not flexible enough to play outside of their lane.

Bottom line: Pro leaders major on the majors, they don't major on the minors. They know what matters most and give their full energy to that. They don't ignore the small things, but keep them in their proper place, in the proper perspective.

Principle Application

1. Look back at your calendar from last week. Consider all your activities and mark them as urgent or important. What is the ratio? Now do it for the last month, for the last quarter, and for the last year. What does the picture look like?

2. Based on this exercise, what would you change or do differently?

3. How can you leverage a negative to make it a positive?

4. What relationship do you have that would benefit from a long-term view?

24 | WIN Today

"You can't manage time, you can only manage your priorities."
—John Maxwell

> **PRO LEADERSHIP PRINCIPLE:** Winning is the result of doing your WIN.

Two years. That is how long it took to write this book. Three years, if you add the year I thought about it after my therapist Bev and my friend Thom challenged me, on separate occasions, to write it. Both had seen and heard me refer to my list: the yellow legal pad in the top drawer of my desk which had two sheets left. Each line contained a sentence; each sentence had ten-words or less. Each sentence contained a lesson life and business had taught me over twenty-five years.

The list started as a private journal, mostly a recording of lessons I had learned—the hard way—ones (in hindsight) I needed to learn but which, as a young leader, I was too insecure to share. I was afraid sharing them would make me look weak or foolish. I did not understand the power of being appropriately vulnerable and how doing so gives impact to one's leadership.

Back then, as a new leader, my leadership goals were so often self-motivated and not others-motivated—inward, not outward. Then, my why was to get the most for *me*, which is a long way from my current why: *to inspire and equip leaders who desire to develop the leader within to become all they were created to be.*

Every so often, I would pull the list out and review it, reflect on the lessons, and sometimes make a note in my journal, adding a thought about its application. Over time, these lessons began to find their way into my leadership—slowly and unintentionally at first, but later, as my experience grew along with the list, I began to use them to help me to inspire and equip the leaders around me.

I knew the lessons were having an impact when I began to hear them repeated back to me by my friends and associates. Lessons I had learned the hard way were helping others so they would not have to pay the high price I did. It turned out the lessons that were being applied were the ones that were actually principles. After all, lessons change, but principles remain the same. Some lessons cannot be applied in any other than specific situations, but principles are true in numerous and varied situations and circumstances.

What finally pushed me to write was the discovery of my why. I realized there were two ways my list could inspire and equip others:

1. if I applied the lessons one-on-one to my own leadership
2. if I wrote them so they could go on without me

Clearly, writing was the best way to reach the most people, to maximize my impact. To have maximum impact on as many people's lives as possible is a desire of my heart. Once my thinking had changed in that direction, it wasn't long before I had to write. But I had never done it before, and my self-belief was low. But the feeling, *I have to do this*, wouldn't go away; instead it grew stronger.

From Dream to Reality

Finally, I moved from, *What if I wrote?* to *How do I do this?* I did some research, I went to a workshop, I read some books, and I spoke to some authors whose work I respected. I put a plan together. Most importantly though, I started writing—just a little at first, but I wrote every day. All the lights weren't green, but I knew one thing, I would never be an author unless I wrote. So, I did.

I will never forget asking my friend, Vince Flynn, how he wrote. He quoted the Stephen King mantra I previously mentioned: "I only write when I am inspired, and I make sure I am inspired every day between 9:30 a.m. and 12:30 p.m."

"Three pages a day, 1,050 words every day, one day at a time—that's how you do it," Vince told me.

Okay, I could do that. So, I started with my list, divided it into three sections and thirty-three chapters, and started writing. I wrote almost every day until I was finished; some days it was easy, some days it was hard, and the most valuable principle was this: winning is the result of doing your WIN daily.

This leadership principle is universal, no matter what size an organization may be. If a leader is going to have impact, she must be disciplined to WIN each day. To do that requires three steps taken daily. If you will commit to these, whether you desire to author a book, build a company or lead an organization, or simply conquer your to-do list, you can achieve your goals, lower the stress of your life, and empower your leadership to have maximum impact. The three-step process is simply this:

1. Plan to WIN.
2. Work your WIN.
3. Refocus on WIN.

By now, if you have taken my previous principles to heart, you have done the work to hammer out who you are, and you have clarified your why. Whether you realize it or not, those two clarifying discoveries are affecting your decision-making. You have a vision, a mission, and a strategic plan with tactical steps to help keep you on the right road.

And now you are in the daily, weekly, and monthly portion of your plan, the pick-and-shovel work. As Stephen Covey so famously wrote in his classic book, *Seven Habits of Highly Effective People*, put first things first. First thing: plan your WIN.

Planning Your WIN

As I've mentioned, my first job after college was as a computer salesman. After completing sales training, I was given two boxes of business cards and told I had ninety days to give them all away—and standing on a street corner passing them out didn't count.

My dad had spent his career in sales management, so I went to him for advice. "How do I do this?" I asked him.

"Make a plan," he responded, "then come and see me." I did. I looked at my territory, ranked the business, and planned my attack—I had one thousand business suspects in my territory, and my goal was to knock on each one of those doors in the next ninety days.

Using the metrics I learned at IBM sales school, 25 percent of my suspects would become prospects and 50 percent of those would make a buy decision in the next twelve months. And, another 50 percent would choose IBM—because, after all, I was selling IBM. That meant I had over sixty-two new customers in my territory, and all I needed to do was find them.

Here was my plan: I would identify thirty businesses each day and, beginning at 9:30 a.m., I would go "door-to-door" until I had met and handed a business card to a decision-maker at each business. That way I could have time for call backs and follow up. My "first thing first" was to find the prospects within the suspect pool.

I went back to Dad, showed him my plan, and asked, "Now what do I do?"

He smiled and said, "Work your plan, then come back to me in ninety days and we can review the results."

I worked the plan and in ninety days I was out of business cards. Ninety days after running out of business cards, I was the number one salesman in the branch. Was I the best salesman? Not by a long shot. I am an experiential learner, so I made about every mistake possible. Was I the smartest salesman? No way. What was it? *I was the most focused and I focused on what was important NOW.* I disciplined myself and led myself so I would not be distracted. This was more easily said than done, as I am dyslexic, which is considered a disability today. However, it was not when I was growing up, so I was forced to learn to deal with what we considered "just another personal tension." The way I learned to discipline myself was one day at a time, focusing on "what is important now" (WIN).

I learned to organize my Mission, my Vision, my Why, and my Strategic Plan into a packet I review weekly, to this day. I do it with a pen in my hand and jot thoughts on it as I review. I revise it annually. What works well for me is an annual plan, although I don't follow the normal calendar year; rather, I start on my birthday and plan the next twelve months. When making my twelve-month plan, I ask one question, "If I am going to accomplish my long-term goals, what needs to be accomplished in the next year?"

Next, I break the year down into three four-month periods—think trimesters.

The world operates in ninety-day periods, but I have found the rhythm that works best for me is one hundred and twenty day periods. If four ninety-day periods work better for you, that's fine; it doesn't matter. After all, time cannot be managed, only spent, so however you find you are most efficient, use that method. The period you choose is a minor not a major; application is what matters most. For this example, I will use trimesters.

So now, plan the upcoming period. Start by asking, *What are the most important goals I need to accomplish during this trimester in order to fulfill my annual plan?* My own trimester goals become a list divided among my various roles and responsibilities. Then, I take that list and make a plan to accomplish each. This helps determine how much time I will need to devote to accomplishing my goals.

For example, to grow my coaching practice requires I stay current with my key referral partners, so I make a plan to accomplish this goal. On the creative side, my goal is to write daily, so I have made a writing plan, spelling out when and what I will write. I also have goals for my personal and professional development, specific goals that require specific actions if I am to accomplish them.

Just as writing daily is a professional goal, reading daily is a personal goal. Leaders are readers, so I must make time and a plan so that I am reading as much and as often as I need to in order to become a broader leader and a better writer. My goal is to read twenty pages a day. I have a book list with books in five categories: History/Biography, Business/Current Affairs, Personal Development, Spiritual Development, and Literature/Fiction/Fun. Undisciplined, I could be thirty pages into a hundred different books. Disciplined, I read five books at a time, one from each category. If I find a book I am interested in reading, it goes on the list where it will wait its turn.

Next is your monthly goals and plan. Weekly planning often multiplies stress, while monthly planning gives margin and reduces stress. If your trimester plan is to succeed, what goals need to be accomplished in the next month? Plan the time and action you will need to take on each and write it down. I have found the one-and-a-half-times (1.5) rule of time helpful in budgeting time needed to accomplish goals. Estimate the amount of time needed to complete a task and multiply it by one and a half. Doing so will build margin into your days and reduce stress, increasing the likelihood you will be able to accomplish your goals.

Next, print a blank calendar page and block your days for the month. I have found the methodology developed by Dan Sullivan for *Strategic Coach* to be effective. In it you have three types of days: free days, focus days, and buffer days. The system is intended to provide balance, giving leaders energy and power which makes them effective.

Free days are fun days where you build energy, you recharge. Focus days are for focusing on the 20 percent of activities that produce 80 percent of your results. Buffer days you work on the 80 percent so you are able to have both free and focus days. One last thing; use the last business day of each month to review and plan the next; for me this is always a buffer day.

Work Your WIN

Step two is easy: go to work and work your WIN. At the end of each day, look at tomorrow and the type of day you planned it to be, then determine WIN.

I have borrowed a tactic from Admiral William McRaven, listing the five most important things to accomplish each day; I call it my "WIN 5." I keep a WIN 5 list on Evernote. Unless and until a task gets to that list, I don't give it any energy.

Coaching tip: your WIN 5 needs to be doable in your day. If you have three meetings, that may be three of your five. Be honest with yourself and use the one-and-a-half-times multiplier to test your WIN 5. Some days you might have a WIN 3 list and some a WIN 1; it doesn't matter. Just don't go more than five. Why? Because even if you have a relatively light day, once you have completed your WIN 5, you now have margin— free space to work on those things that are often hard to get to, because while they are important, they are not urgent. Those things go onto my *Buffer List*, a list I pull up whenever I have completed my daily WIN list.

Refocus on WIN

Finally, a nod to reality. Leadership and life are full of distractions, and a pro leader must learn to refocus; often you must refocus many times in a day to win.

Tiger Woods is arguably the greatest golfer to ever play the game, not only that but in a recent survey he is the most recognized person in the world. Recently, I watched a documentary on Woods, *Chasing 82*, aired on the Golf Channel. It is essentially a highlight reel of his eighty-one career victories and his quest to match or beat Sam Snead's record eighty-two career victories, the most in the history of professional golf.

The show was on while I was working out, and it was fun to watch, but what struck me was what so many of his peers believed to be the strength of Tiger's game and the reason behind his success: Tiger had an ability to focus that few have ever possessed. Mental discipline in combination with extraordinary athletic giftedness has resulted in eighty-two (so far) victories.

I truly believe that focus combined with competence determines one's level of success. I would add one other thing: attitude. Although it wasn't mentioned about Tiger, if you listened to his interviews, you heard the attitude of a winner. As one of his peers said when asked what it was like to compete with him, "You knew he could beat you, he knew he could beat you, and he knew you knew he could beat you."

How about you, my reader? By now, I hope you have developed a winning attitude (even if you didn't start with one), and a growing level of competence. Now, what will take you to the next level of pro leadership is your ability to focus—your mental toughness. Leadership is a marathon, not a sprint. To succeed you will need to maintain your focus (and refocus) over long periods of time.

Try this: take forty-five minutes on the weekend to review your Vision, your Why, your Mission, and your Strategic Goals: annual, trimester, and month. Make some notes; remind yourself of your WIN. Refocus. Do this exercise weekly, and over time, I believe you will be empowered by it. Plus, it will give you margin, because you will no longer need to think about your WIN. With this repetition, it will find its way into your subconscious and, as a result, you will be naturally guided to WIN. When that happens, winning will surely follow and your leadership will have impact.

You will have become a *pro leader.*

Principle Application

1. What is your number one priority?

2. What percentage of your time did you spend on it last week?

3. How do you decide where to spend your time?

4. What are the "big rocks" you need to move?

5. What are the "little rocks" you need to clear out of the way?

6. How does the 80:20 principle relate to your leadership?

AFTERWORD

I have always thought Vespas were cool, and I have often imagined myself riding one. I have known a handful of people who have owned them and have liked them all. It must be something about the personality of the Vespa owners I know that attracts me to them: all are leaders, they are individualists, they are independent, and they enjoy life.

So not surprisingly, as I walked into a nearby Starbucks recently, I paused for a moment to admire the grey Vespa parked on the sidewalk just outside the door. I was there for a meeting with an entrepreneurial leader whom I had gotten to know when we'd done some business together as I was forming my holding company a few years ago. Matt had just launched a software company built around a platform to help in the corporate event planning space. I loved his vision, his energy, and his focus. He clearly had entrepreneurial DNA. I thought he had a great idea too, but, not being familiar with his industry, I did not believe I could help, so I introduced him to a friend who ran a private equity fund with a software focus.

My desire to meet with Matt was driven by my own "why": *to inspire and equip leaders who desire to develop the leader within, so they may become all they were created to be.* Matt and people like him are why I founded Andrew Wyatt Leadership and why I wrote this book. It's what gets me out of bed each morning. I love leadership development, especially one-on-one coaching, whether a formal client relationship or a casual one, like my meeting with Matt. After thirty years of relentless focus on my bottom line, I find it fun to be focused on someone else's.

Fast forward eighteen months. I had not seen or spoken with Matt since I'd referred him on to someone else and was curious about how things had turned out. So, I set up a "catch-up" meeting at Starbucks, half-way between our offices. It was a crisp, fall day, and I walked in sporting my favorite attire: jeans, grey t-shirt, Red Wing shoes, and my black Patagonia puffer vest. The first person I noticed when I walked in was Matt, and it was as if I was back in seventh grade and I had called him and we had decided what to wear. It was good for a laugh.

We sat down together and he caught me up over a grande chai tea latte. The software idea had not worked; he'd pulled the plug when he realized he did not have the resources to bring it to the finish line. But he wasn't discouraged; rather, that road had led him to a new opportunity where he was working in his strengths and growing significantly in the process. Balance was being restored to his life. He was growing as a leader and he said to me, "I cannot believe how valuable that experience was. I already can see new opportunities. I love what I'm doing now."

I, too, love what I am doing today, I have gained a lot of wisdom in my life of leadership, and it is rewarding to pass it on and to help others as they grow. My "why" is the outcome of my governing belief: without leadership nothing happens. Strong, caring, servant leaders are good leaders and good leaders produce good outcomes. Being invited into leaders' lives to help them grow and develop in this way is such a privilege.

As we walked out of Starbucks forty-five minutes later, Matt smiled broadly, shook my hand, and thanked me for reaching out to him. Then, he stopped right next to the Vespa and said, "You're a natural coach; it's the perfect business for you. Thanks for your help."

With that, he jumped on his Vespa and rode away.

ABOUT THE AUTHOR

 Andy Wyatt is a world-class business leader and sought-after coach and speaker. He founded his most recent company, Andrew Wyatt Leadership, with a desire to inspire and equip people to develop the leader within, so they can become all they were created to be.

He began this work after completing twenty-four years as founder and CEO of Cornerstone Capital Management LLC, which began as a private wealth management business in 1993 and grew into an institution asset manager with over fifteen billion dollars in assets under management. The story of that enterprise is in this book.

Andy has been married to his wife Luann for thirty-three years and they have three grown children: Claire, Joe, and Maggie. He also has a West Highland white terrier named Winnie. They make their home in Minneapolis, Minnesota.

www.andrewwyattleadership.com
www.proleadership.net

CPSIA information can be obtained
at www.ICGtesting.com
Printed in the USA
JSHW041135220321
12783JS00002B/202